D1560837

This book belongs to

----------------------------------------

----------------------------------------

----------------------------------------

# Snail Mail

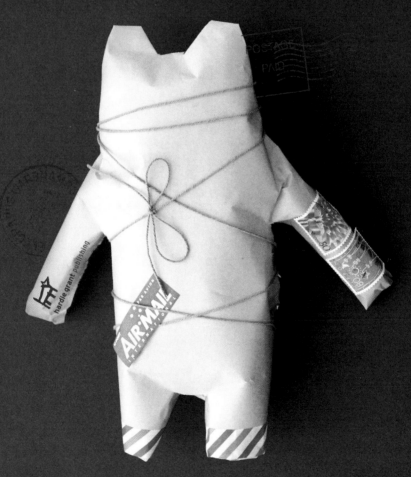

MICHELLE MACKINTOSH

snail mail
/sneɪl meɪl/ (say 'snayl mayl)
*noun* the ordinary post,
as opposed to email.

CONTENTS

¥357

If you are reading this book then, like me, you probably feel that the romance of handwritten letters is not only alive and well, but more important than ever!

Where some people get their kicks from Twitter or Facebook, I have always loved letters and the personal nature of 'analogue' correspondence. I love how instantly recognisable handwriting is – the way it could only be written by the sender – and how there can be mistakes, flaws and slip-ups that can't just be amended by the backspace bar.

Reading the letters my great-grandmother sent across the seas to her mother and siblings was my first taste of the mystery and nostalgia of different places and times. The handwriting was so beautiful, and the language that she used to write to her loved ones was so caring, kind and considerate.

When you think about it, a letter is a pretty complex piece of social history. The postage stamp gives a letter its time and place, and the stamp design reflects the important people, trends, styles and colours of the time. The letters you send and receive reveal a lot about you: are your postcards placed in envelopes or left free for the postman to read? Is your handwriting small or large, and do you like to use coloured pens?

Writing letters as a teenager put me on the path to become a designer. When I was in high school I had an extended stay in hospital, and my connection to the outside world was through the post. I spent hours intricately decorating the envelopes and perfecting my handwriting, and it was at this point I realised I wanted to draw and create for a living. While I was at home convalescing, a letter in the mail brightened my day and took my mind off being sick.

It's amazing how much of an emotional impact letters can have – perhaps more than anything we might tweet or share online. Before my father died, he wrote me a letter to be read once he passed away; I wouldn't open it for ten years. I couldn't bear the thought that this would be the last piece of correspondence I'd have from him. He had incredibly distinctive handwriting, and I felt comforted by the sealed letter, a constant reminder of his presence.

While much of today's communication is instant, thoughtful letter-writing should take time. An important letter almost always requires effort, whether it's in the form of research or time spent perfecting the prose and handwriting. After all, that love letter you're labouring over could be stashed under your first love's bed, waiting to be re-read in twenty years' time. Or that condolence card you sent to a friend could be placed in a beautiful box and treasured as an important keepsake.

With this in mind, I decided to put together some ideas on how to express yourself through correspondence and get the most out of old-school letter-writing. I hope you will find some inspiration in these pages and fall in love with writing and making things for the people you love the most.

This book is all about starting a slow correspondence revolution. Not everything needs to be 'right now' or 'I need it tomorrow'. Letters take time to write and decorate. They also take time to arrive, and the anticipation is such an important and powerful thing. And they are worth the wait. After all, they can be kept and treasured forever.

With love
Michelle

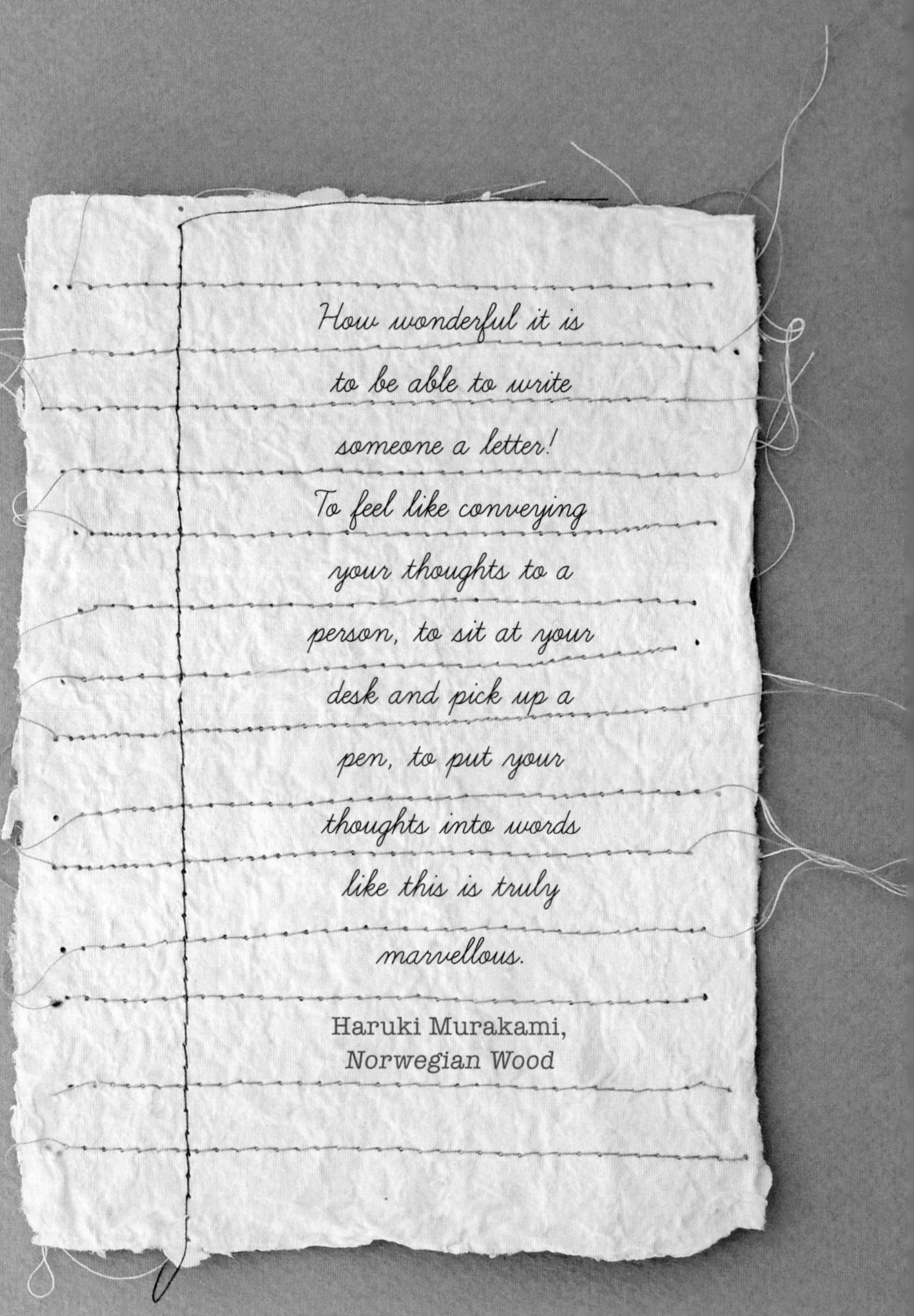

*How wonderful it is*

*to be able to write*

*someone a letter!*

*To feel like conveying*

*your thoughts to a*

*person, to sit at your*

*desk and pick up a*

*pen, to put your*

*thoughts into words*

*like this is truly*

*marvellous.*

Haruki Murakami,
Norwegian Wood

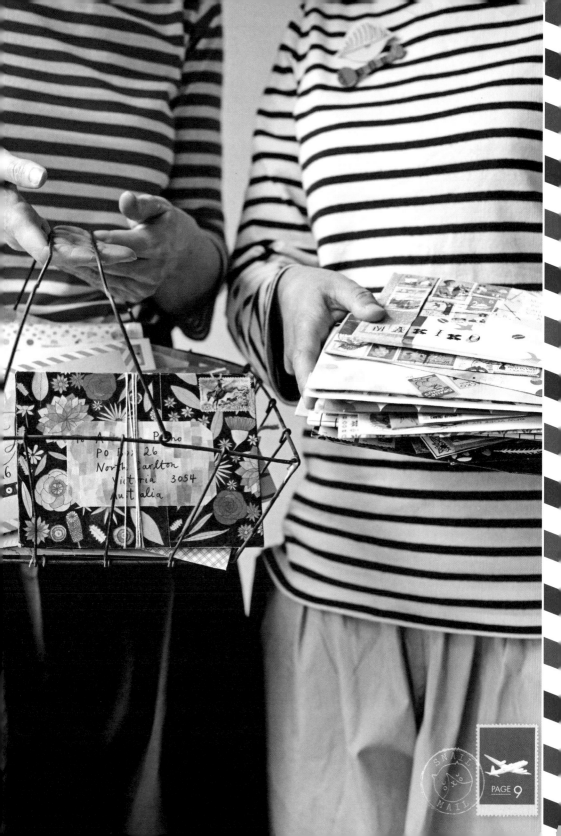

# THE LOST ART OF MANNERS

I love to travel to Tokyo at least three times a year, and the kindness and exquisite manners of the Japanese people I meet is one of the reasons I keep going back. The way Japanese culture weaves thoughtfulness and beauty into the ordinary is endlessly inspiring to me, and is something that really got me thinking about manners and what they mean in the twenty-first century. Japan has so many stores dedicated to papercraft because being creative with correspondence is part of everyday life, with letters and notes exchanged to express all kinds of sentiments. It made me wonder why this part of our culture is rare these days and how it's all linked to kindness, manners and etiquette.

Manners and etiquette used to be a serious business. They were the subject of best-selling books and many popular magazine columns. Nowadays, however, many of the intricacies of polite society have been lost. For whatever reason, it seems like teaching etiquette is not much of a priority anymore – or at least, no-one is quite sure who should be responsible for it. It's surprising to hear the opinions that different generations have on the matter. Should it be family, school or religion that teaches us manners? Or is it books, television and movies? Do we learn by observing what not to do, or should we be proactive and lay down rules?

At their core, manners are all about everyday kindness and respect. A thoughtful gesture, a simple please or thank you: in my experience, it's these everyday kindnesses that make life worth living. And any relationship, household, school or workplace needs a healthy dose of respect to function properly. Bad manners lead to dysfunction, and good manners can help amend challenging situations.

This book is not meant to be a morality lesson, but it will show you some ways to bring a bit of thoughtfulness into your everyday life. Sending a letter to say thank you, or to celebrate success, or just because you are thinking about someone, will brighten the recipient's day. And it will brighten yours, too.

> Minding your manners gives you opportunities to send snail mail!

**TELEGRAM**

## A LETTER OF THANKS

Whatever the occasion, saying 'thank you' is always a nice thing to do. Try sending one ...

* to a prospective employer after a job interview, to say you appreciated the opportunity to be interviewed (it could even improve your chances!);
* to someone who picks your kids up from school, collects your mail while you are on holidays, or performs any other sort of everyday kindness;
* to your child's teacher, sports coach or mentor;
* to nurses and doctors who cared for you or your loved one;
* or even to your host after a nice dinner.

## A LETTER OF APOLOGY

If you have done the wrong thing, 'sorry' is a small word with a big impact.

* Write as sincerely as possible. This sort of letter requires some serious thought, and the self-reflection is good for you, too.

## A LETTER OF RECONCILIATION

It's all too easy to damage relationships with other people, but in many cases we can and should salvage them.

* Everyone is human; we say and do the wrong thing sometimes. Writing with sincerity can help you make amends.
* Even if you don't hear back from the recipient, you will feel better knowing you wrote something heartfelt.
* A letter simply saying 'I miss you' can go a long way.

**TELEGRAM    TELEGRAM**

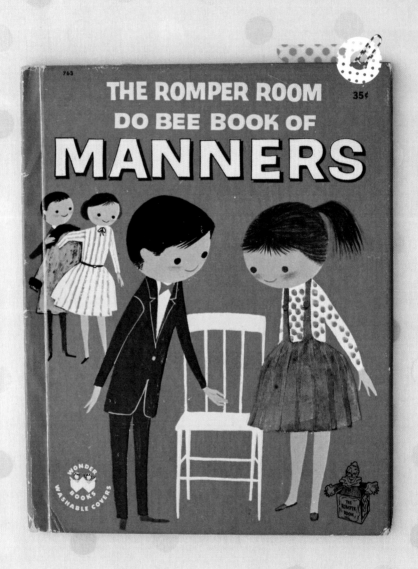

THE ROMPER ROOM
DO BEE BOOK OF
MANNERS

763

35¢

WONDER
BOOKS
WASHABLE COVERS

Tuesday 11th March 2014

My Dearest Miss Macintosh,

It has been to long since our last meeting and I look forward to seeing you soon. I have booked the coach for this Friday and will travel light so as to make it a quick day down.

I do appologize, my quill is quit worn and have not been to my local man to aquire some more.

You must write me and tell me of the weather so i will know what to pack for my season in the city.

I can report that the project is going very well, there is only four more drawings to complete, potatatoe, beans, mushroo and some off the garden utensils, oh a Kale, i must confess to putting that of it will be very hard to reproduce scene with persevterance i will pres

The weather as i write you of perfect, a light breeze, sun sh a care in the world no aw slow one down.

My walk this m ng the prominade was very the oce so good i changed boxes a a dip, so very refreshing

Too short, I must close of i m the mail coach to hope fully reach you fine

Fondest Regards Miss Menzies. X X

# ANALOGUE VS DIGITAL

*Lessons from the handwritten age*

// In today's world of instant communication – texting, Facebook, Twitter and other social media – have we lost the art of truly personal correspondence?

// Not so long ago, the way you spoke or wrote to a close friend or colleague was not the way you spoke or wrote to an authority figure. But digital communication has made it easier than ever to bring all facets of our lives together.

// As a consequence, we speak to family, friends, acquaintances and colleagues in the same voice – whether it's passively, through social media, or directly, through group correspondence – raising questions about tone, content and the sort of language you use to speak to different age and social groups. Using the one voice to talk to a group of varied people can leave recipients feeling hurt, left out or just confused.

// The way we present ourselves online can have real-life consequences, too. Many employers now seek out a job applicant's online profile before asking them in for an interview – as do prospective dates! So think twice before posting pictures from that mad party, or having a public conversation about someone's erratic behaviour. Some things are best kept to private communication: an email, a letter, or a face-to-face conversation.

// We can all learn a little about handling the digital world from old-school analogue correspondence. After all, they're not so far removed from each other! You could even say that the postcard, with its glamorous photograph and sender's caption for all to see, was the first piece of social media; the telegram, an ancestor of the tweet.

// So before you hit 'send' next time, take a moment to consider your words as if you'd written them down in a letter you were about to send. Is the tone appropriate for everyone who will see it? Does it contain material that is best kept private? And most importantly, will you regret sending or posting it later?

TELEGRAPH OFFICE
2 9 SEP 1961
THORNBURY N. 17. VIC.

MARLENE CANN
34 FYFFE STREET
THORNBURY VIC

TELEGRA
THORNBURY N. 17. VIC.

TY 063= NC10 087  ASXE 154  RE
ADEALIDE SUB 12 2.47P
Adelaide Sub

MARLENE CANN /s
34 FIFFE ST
NORTHCOTE VIC ( THORNBURY )

ARRIVED SAFELY MISSING YOU LOVE.
(34) 20

TO EXPEDITE DELIVERY
ADDRESS TELE

PLEASE POST YOUR MAIL
EARLY IN THE DAY

SNAIL
MAIL

PAGE 15

## OPEN COMMUNICATION

### POSTCARDS AND SOCIAL MEDIA

I have always been interested in how open postcards are. The postie can read your card – and so can your family, flatmates or friends! The sender faces an interesting dilemma: should the postcard be written in a personal way, or should it be kept purely factual? It should come as no surprise, then, that the postcard has given rise to so many clichés and commonplace, reveal-nothing expressions like 'Wish you were here', 'Having an amazing time' or even 'Weather's great, wish you were here' (and its humorous cousin, 'Weather's here, wish you were great').

It's a good example of how some things never change. Before the internet, when friends and family were abroad, we couldn't truly gauge what sort of a holiday they were having from what was written on a postcard. Likewise, on social media you will be hard-pressed to find anyone talking about their miserable trip full of upset stomachs and muggings. It's something that makes me ponder our online existence: how many tweets and status updates reveal only part of the truth, and how many the full truth? And which is healthier?

### TELEGRAMS AND TWITTER

Because each word cost money, telegrams were typically short. Twitter works in a similar way, with its 140-character limit responsible for each tweet's brevity, rather than dollars and cents. Whether it's a tweet or a telegram, the writer has to get pretty creative to deliver something punchy or meaningful in a few well-chosen words. Both mediums are forms of quick correspondence, although telegrams were pretty much always used for urgent matters. It would probably be fair to say that most tweets involve highly 'non-urgent' matters – unless what so-and-so ate for lunch is your highest priority!

*Was the postcard the first piece of social media and the telegram the first tweet?*

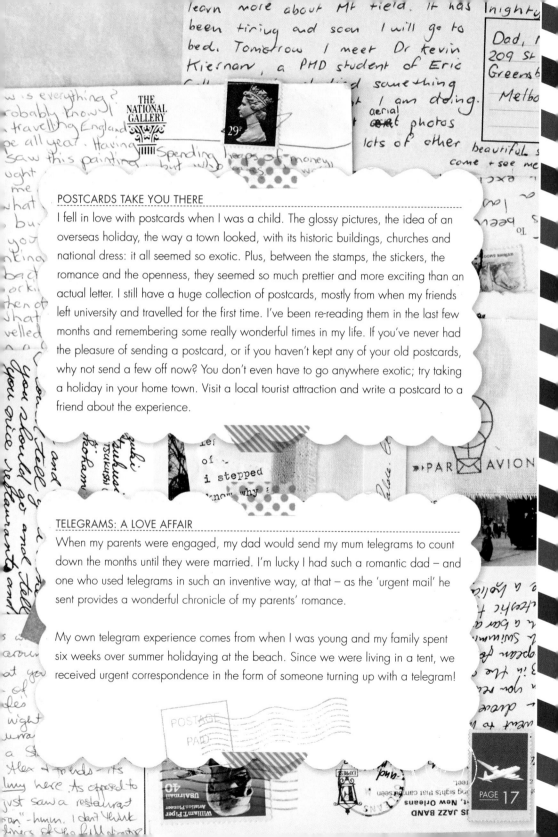

## POSTCARDS TAKE YOU THERE

I fell in love with postcards when I was a child. The glossy pictures, the idea of an overseas holiday, the way a town looked, with its historic buildings, churches and national dress: it all seemed so exotic. Plus, between the stamps, the stickers, the romance and the openness, they seemed so much prettier and more exciting than an actual letter. I still have a huge collection of postcards, mostly from when my friends left university and travelled for the first time. I've been re-reading them in the last few months and remembering some really wonderful times in my life. If you've never had the pleasure of sending a postcard, or if you haven't kept any of your old postcards, why not send a few off now? You don't even have to go anywhere exotic; try taking a holiday in your home town. Visit a local tourist attraction and write a postcard to a friend about the experience.

## TELEGRAMS: A LOVE AFFAIR

When my parents were engaged, my dad would send my mum telegrams to count down the months until they were married. I'm lucky I had such a romantic dad – and one who used telegrams in such an inventive way, at that – as the 'urgent mail' he sent provides a wonderful chronicle of my parents' romance.

My own telegram experience comes from when I was young and my family spent six weeks over summer holidaying at the beach. Since we were living in a tent, we received urgent correspondence in the form of someone turning up with a telegram!

*Have the clichés so often used in circulars and open letters twisted and changed and popped up in a brand-new way on social media?*

## LETTIQUETTE AND NETIQUETTE

### SENDING AND RECEIVING LETTERS COMES WITH ITS OWN ETIQUETTE

* The only time it's OK to read someone's mail is if it's a postcard on the fridge.
* If a friend shares with you the contents of a letter, do not share it with others.
* Steaming open someone else's correspondence is never OK.
* Always put your return address on the back of the envelope.
* Be kind to the postie by making your handwriting legible.
* Always remember to include the postcode or zipcode when writing the address on your envelope.

### JUST LIKE SNAIL MAIL, THE DIGITAL WORLD HAS ITS OWN SET OF RULES

* Reading an email, text message, instant message or other private online communication not meant for you is never OK.
* Consider the tone of your message before you send it out to a group.
* Remember that your public comments on friends' social media pages can be read by everyone in that friendship group, so be mindful of the group dynamic and other people's feelings.
* An online circle of friends that includes family, friends and school or work colleagues may be the wrong forum for anything other than general comments.
* If anyone tries to engage online with you in a negative or aggressive way, don't bite back.
* If you're going to send group emails, break it down into smaller groups. Email your family, your colleagues and your different friendship groups separately. Within each smaller group, if possible, address each recipient by name.
* While convenient, group emails can be a bit impersonal. I always like to apologise for having to resort to sending a group message.
* Always try to promptly reply to emails from friends, family members and work colleagues. If you can't reply straight away, try to reply within forty-eight hours.
* 'Unfriending' is just as ugly as it sounds. Use it only in the most dire circumstances.

These days,
we are quite unaccustomed
to putting pen to paper: texting,
social media and email rule our
communication world. So I can't blame
you if you haven't the foggiest idea of where
to start! I think the best way to dip your toe
into the letter-writing pool is to choose an
occasion or reason to write and go from
there. In this chapter, you'll find some
of the best 'whens' to write a letter,
as well as some helpful language
tips if your vocabulary contains
too many abbreviations ...

# 1.
# Write here, right now

A letter always

seemed to me

like immortality

because it is

the mind alone

without

corporeal friend.

Emily Dickinson

This is the ultimate happy mail. Over the top IS recommended

Make an envelope that's bright, fun and perhaps unexpected!

It's time to celebrate with some seriously pretty mail

CONGRATULATIONS
*letters*

| | Your friend's achievement should be celebrated properly | | Enthusiasm is infectious | ✔ | Be proud! | ⟫→ |
|---|---|---|---|---|---|---|
| | | | Good news should be shared | ◁))) | Have fun creating | |
| | | | Make a date to celebrate in person | 🍸 | Toast them! | |

# WHEN TO WRITE: CELEBRATION AND GOOD TIMES

## BIG AND SMALL OCCASIONS

When your loved one is going through or has achieved something exciting, a letter is a lovely way to mark a success or a happy occasion. Remember, what is small to one person is big to another, so get with the making and sending, and let someone know you are thinking of them.

Small achievements are some of the best reasons to send snail mail. The recipient won't be expecting anything, and they can't not be delighted when a cute letter arrives addressed to them in the mail.

Simple words like 'I'm proud of you', 'I knew you could do it' or 'This is such an achievement, well done' will put a smile on your loved one's face. After all, you *are* proud of them, and you want them to feel special!

## SOMETHING TO CELEBRATE!

If you can't be there in person for a loved one's special occasion, why not send your congratulations and best wishes in the mail? You can still be part of the event by sending a piece of memorable communication.

Sometimes it can seem like there is not a lot to celebrate, and sometimes life becomes so busy that we forget to mark occasions properly. But there are so many fun opportunities to send a letter or card or parcel in the mail: births, birthdays, promotions, weddings, housewarmings, graduations and more!

One of my favourite occasions to send a card is a child's first day of school. Another is to congratulate someone on a really wonderful piece of work they have just completed. Whatever the event or occasion, take some time and make something really pretty. You may just start a snail mail revolution!

Poets don't draw.
They unravel their
handwriting and
then tie it up again,
but differently.
Jean Cocteau

Try collaging some imagery of your idol

Use stickers, badges or any of their merchandise

Make a few versions before you settle on the real thing

| | Maximum effort equals maximum impact so go for it | | Create to be seen | Take a photo of your creation |
|---|---|---|---|---|
| | | Own the fanboy/fangirl title | | Practise your prose |
| | | Turn your obsession into letter art! | | Make it bold |

# WHEN TO WRITE: FAN MAIL

## FANBOY, FANGIRL

Do you have a music crush on a popstar, a creative crush on an artist, or an inspirational crush on a TV or radio personality? Why not send them a letter explaining what they, or their art or music, mean to you?

If you're worried about coming across all stalker-y, don't be: so long as you keep it reasonable, letting someone know you think they are amazing is one of the nicest reasons to write a letter, and I expect reading such a letter is pretty nice, too. Don't forget, before social media, fan clubs that relied on snail mail played an important role for bands and actors who wanted to connect with their audiences.

There are a few important rules to note, however. Remember, you do not know the recipient of your letter, so keep it complimentary and fun. No need to go over the top here (see coming across as stalker-y above), unless you want the police knocking on your door at an ungodly hour. By all means send a bit of fan art, but mailing body parts is not a sign of undying love – it's one of mental instability.

Instead, talk about what their art means to you. You can even thank them for helping you get through tough times, or talk about how when you see them on television or hear their music, it makes you smile. On no account should you ask for a meet-up time or date, or ask them if they are single. This means you've crossed over to stalker territory. And you'll only be disappointed by the lack of reply.

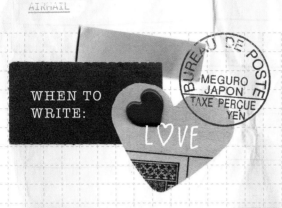

## WHEN TO WRITE: LOVE

High emotions always accompany the writing of a love letter. You want to tell your lover how you are feeling, but don't want to appear flippant, naff or cringe-worthily romantic! You want to write something down, but you can't find the words ... it's enough to give you palpitations! But don't panic just yet. Take your time and you'll soon find that a love letter is the best way to say things you have trouble articulating in reality. This is the most intimate form of correspondence, for two people alone to share. So make it count!

♥ One of the best reasons to write to your lover is if you are separated. Things can get pretty lonely if you are working or holidaying away from your paramour, or one of you may feel left out or left behind. A love letter from a distant city brings you closer together. Write your correspondence on a drink coaster from a place you've visited, or stationery from your hotel room, or any kind of paraphernalia that will make your dearest feel included in your experience.

♥ If you are lucky enough to be somewhere picturesque, sending a lot of postcards can also be romantic. One sent every day or every couple of days, with just a few heartfelt lines about how you miss your beloved, will make them feel loved and included – not to mention they will be awaiting your return with anticipation!

♥ Even if you are not separated from your sweetheart, a letter is a wonderful way to express how you feel about them – something you may be frightened to unleash, but should. Remember, love letters can become treasured keepsakes or burnt in a rage, but either way, intense emotions are involved! If your words could possibly go up in smoke, you may as well make the best love letter anyone has ever made!

Use some
upcycled papers
and washi tapes

Buy a lovely pen
and practise your
best handwriting

At the post office, ask
to see their limited
edition stamps

|  It doesn't matter who you are. We all love a love letter! |  | Send your LL rain, hail or shine!  |
|---|---|---|
| | Make it personal  | Keep it simple  Well done |
| | Decorate the envelope and have fun making it!  | |

romantic cards don't have to be daggy or naff

Spray your love letter with your perfume or a familiar scent that is meaningful to both of you. For instance, if your first date was at the cinema, try immersing your letter in some oil-free, air-popped popcorn for a few days before sending it.

don't disappoint! cute up your letters so the contents deliver on the anticipation of opening

## A FEW NOTES ON WRITING A LOVE LETTER

* Make up your own rules. Write an essay if you feel inspired, but a few beautiful lines go a long way, too.

* Ensure you and the recipient are on the same page regarding your relationship. There is a fine line between declaring love and stalking, so make sure you don't cross it.

* If your paramour is a multi-tasker who may not read past the first paragraph in one sitting, providing a hook or a suggestion of intimacy every couple of sentences will keep them reading on.

* Above everything else, love letters need to be highly personal. Anything too general could give the impression you have written the same letter to multiple people. You don't want to sound like a love robot!

* Having trouble capturing your thoughts and feelings in a letter that strikes the right chord? Try using song lyrics from both of your favourite bands.

* In the past, love letters were often encrypted, written in code, invisible ink, or a secret or foreign language. Why not try some of these old-school techniques, especially if you're worried about someone steaming your letters open? Diluted lemon juice used as ink remains invisible until heated gently over a lightbulb.

* Avoid creating any grammatic tension! If your lover is a stickler for spelling and grammar, make sure your letter is mistake-free. One misplaced comma or unconjugated verb could spell disaster. You don't want your relationship to be known as the Comedy of Errors!

* If you feel like you lack the writing skills, why not illustrate your sentiments? As long as you keep those heartfelt personal feelings in there somewhere, even stick figures will do. It's also a great way to thread a bit of humour through your correspondence if your sweetheart loves to laugh.

A love letter from
Robert Browning
to his future wife,
Elizabeth Barrett

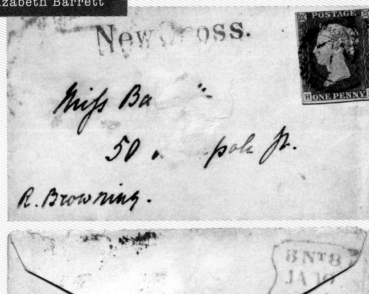

ah - so into me has it gone, and part of
me has it become, this great living poetry
of yours, not a flower of which but I
took root and grew in oh, how different
that is from lying to be dried and pressed
flat and prized highly and put in a book
with a proper account at top and bottom,
and shut up and put away... and the book
called a "Flora", besides! After all, I need
not give up the thought of
doing that, too, in time; because even
now, talking with whoever is worthy,
I can give a reason for my faith
in one and another excellence,
the fresh strange music, the affluent
language, the exquisite pathos and
true new brave thought - but in
this addressing myself to you, your

own self, and for the first time,
my feeling rises altogether -
I do, as I say, love these Books
with all my heart - and I love
you too: do you know I was
once not very far from seeing
in really seeing you, and Mr Kenyon
said to me one morning "would
you like to see Miss Barrett?"
- then he went to announce me,
- then he returned... you were too
unwell - and now it is years
ago - and I feel as at some untoward passage in my travels
- as if I had been close, so close, to
some world's-wonder in chapel

or crypt, only a screen to push
and I might have entered - but
there was some slight as it now
seems, slight and just-sufficient
bar to admission, and the half-
opened door shut, and I went
home my thousands of miles,
and the sight was - never to be!

Well, these Poems were to be -
and this time thankful joy and
pride with which I feel myself
Yours ever faithfully,
Robert Browning.

New Cross, Hatcham, Surrey.

I love your verses with all my heart, dear
Miss Barrett, - and this is no off-hand complimentary letter that I shall write, whatever
else, no prompt matter-of-course recognition
of your genius and here a graceful and natural end of the thing: since the day last week
when I first read your poems, I quite laugh
to remember how I have been turning and
turning again in my mind what I should
be able to tell you of their effect upon me
for in the first flush of delight I thought
I would this once get out of my habit of
purely passive enjoyment, when I do really
enjoy, and thoroughly justify my admiration - perhaps even, as a loyal fellow-
craftsman should, try and find fault and
do you some little good to be proud of
hereafter! - but nothing comes of it

New Cross, Hatcham, Surrey.

I love your verses with all my heart, dear Miss Barrett, – and this is no off-hand complimentary letter that I shall write, – whatever else, no prompt matter-of-course recognition of your genius and there a graceful and natural end of the thing: since the day last week when I first read your poems, I quite laugh to remember how I have been turning and turning again in my mind what I should be able to tell you of their effect upon me – for in the first flush of delight I thought I would this once get out of my habit of purely passive enjoyment, when I do really enjoy, and thoroughly justify my admiration – perhaps even, as a loyal fellow-craftsman should, try and find fault and do you some little good to be proud of hereafter! – but nothing comes of it all – so into me has it gone, and part of me has it become, this great living poetry of yours, not a flower of which but took root and grew ... oh, how different that is from lying to be dried and pressed flat and prized highly and put in a book with a proper account at top and bottom, and shut up and put away ... and the book called a "Flora," besides!

After all, I need not give up the thought of doing that, too, in time; because even now, talking with whoever is worthy, I can give a reason for my faith in one and another excellence, the fresh strange music, the affluent language, the exquisite pathos and true new brave thought – but in this addressing myself to you, your own self, and for the first time, my feeling rises altogether.

I do, as I say, love these Books with all my heart – and I love you too: do you know I was once not very far from seeing ... really seeing you? Mr Kenyon said to me one morning "would you like to see Miss Barrett?" – then he went to announce me, – then he returned ... you were too unwell – and now it is years ago – and I feel as at some untoward passage in my travels – as if I had been close, so close, to some world's-wonder in chapel or crypt, ... only a screen to push and I might have entered – but there was some slight ... so it now seems ... slight and just-sufficient bar to admission, and the half-opened door shut, and I went home my thousands of miles, and the sight was never to be! Well, these Poems were to be – and this true thankful joy and pride with which I feel myself

Yours ever faithfully,
Robert Browning.

## GETTING SERIOUS WITH YOUR LOVE LETTER

The love letter is the ultimate in personal correspondence. It's the most intimate and highly sought-after letter one can receive. It should be taken seriously!

Choose some special paper or make a card. Write a draft or drafts before you commit to your final letter. Select an interesting pen to write with, one that accentuates your handwriting style. Finish it off with a spray of perfume, a pressed flower or something else that reminds your lover of you.

First impressions count, so purchase or make an interesting envelope. Write your lover's name and address with great care. Decorate accordingly and don't forget to ask the post office if there are any interesting or special edition stamps to choose from.

Now post your letter and forget about it! Remember, this is the slow art of communication, so you may not get a reply or acknowledgement of its delivery for a while. Give the recipient time to read and digest your turn of phrase and romantic declarations.

*I never
should have
said, the books that
you read, were all
I loved you for*
The Sundays

*I love you
from the bottom
of my pencil case*
The Beautiful
South

## MAKING DECLARATIONS OF LOVE A CASUAL AFFAIR

Approach online public declarations of love with caution! Yes, it may be nice to show your friends and acquaintances how much you adore or are adored. But this form of correspondence can fall flat if the relationship does not work out, or if the declaration of love is not reciprocated. Even worse, it can turn into an online squabble involving ex-partners who are still in your friendship group!

Carefully consider how much intimate information you share online – and with whom you share it. When posted online, messages of love and affection, something once sacred and preciously written, can easily be accessed and shared by anyone. Do your parents, your boss, and even friends who are going through a difficult break-up *really* need to read your passionate love notes?

The skies above are blue.
My heart was wrapped up in clover.
The night I looked at you
Etta James

Kiss me properly and pull me apart
The Last Shadow Puppets

Canberra City **TRAVELODGE**

CNR. NORTHBOURNE AVE.
& COOYONG STREET
TEL: 49 6911, P.O. BOX 8...
CANBERRA CITY

PHONE 5.

**Coach House MOTOR INN**

**COACH HOUSE MOTOR INN**
END STREET, DENILIQUIN • PHONE DENILIQUIN 1001-2-3

**Coach House MOTOR INN**

**COACH HOUSE MOTOR INN**
END STREET, DENILIQUIN • PHONE DENILIQUIN 1001-2-3

*Commodore*
**MOTEL**
CNR. TIMOR & KEPLER STREETS
WARRNAMBOOL

MEENI
MOTEL

SNAIL MAIL

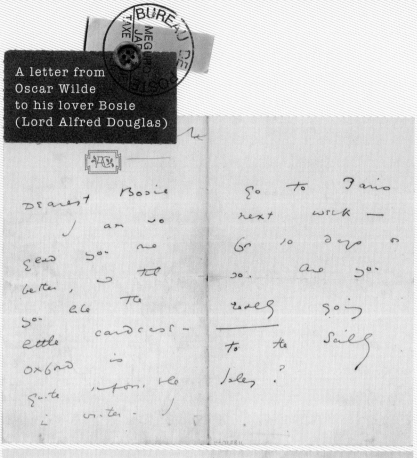

A letter from
Oscar Wilde
to his lover Bosie
(Lord Alfred Douglas)

Dearest Bosie

I am so glad you are better, and that you like the little cardcase—Oxford is quite impossible in winter. I go to Paris next week—for 10 days or so. Are you really going to the Scilly Isles?

I should awfully like to go away with you somewhere—where it is hot and coloured—

I am terribly busy in town—Tree rushing up to see me on all occasions—also strange and troubling personalities walking in painted pageants—

Of the poem I will write tomorrow.

Ever yours
Oscar

Plan your letter as soon as you hear the sad news

Choose colours you know your loved one will respond to

Keep the styling of your envelope gentle and thoughtful

GRIEF letters

Don't expect an answer to this kind of letter

Offer help and support with everyday life »→

Make it heartfelt ⊠ Be genuine ⧖ Don't push

Make sure you keep in contact 🕅 Listen! Be kind

## WHEN TO WRITE: CONSOLATION AND HARD TIMES

While we all hope that our lives are filled with happy moments, sad moments are inescapable. One of the most important letters you can write is a letter to a loved one when they have lost someone special. Don't worry if you don't know what to say or how to act. It's making the effort to comfort that counts.

My father passed away when I was quite young, and I was so surprised at the way people around me handled the situation and my grief. One thing that happened was people started giving me advice that, while well-intentioned, was mostly inappropriate or at times quite hurtful. The other thing that happened was people stopped communicating with me, I suppose because they were frightened of saying the wrong thing, or because they just didn't know how to handle the situation. For me, it all led to a pretty isolating experience. What helped save me from feeling completely alone, and what I appreciated the most, were the handwritten letters and cards I received. I still have all of these today – they have been read and re-read – and they still give me great comfort.

### A SMALL RAY OF SUNSHINE

There's nothing you can say or do to take away your loved one's pain, but you can brighten their day with a piece of mail. A letter or card can be read in their own time. Most importantly, it doesn't need to be answered. It will not ask questions or add pressure. It simply exists to show the recipient that they are in your thoughts.

Remember that grief is, unfortunately, a long-term kind of arrangement. Do your best to help your loved one feel loved and supported long after the funeral is over. A card in the mail on the anniversary of a death, or a care package (see Chapter 4) at any time can let a loved one know that you really care.

Every one can master a grief but
he that has it.

William Shakespeare

It's so curious: one can resist
tears and 'behave' very well in the
hardest hours of grief. But then
someone makes you a friendly
sign behind a window, or one notices
that a flower that was in
bud only yesterday has suddenly
blossomed, or a letter slips from a
drawer ... and everything collapses.

Colette

## A FEW NOTES ON WRITING TO A GRIEVING LOVED ONE

* Simple is best.
* Avoid clichés or the kind of statement that tells your loved one what to do (for example, 'You'll feel better soon!' or 'In time these feelings will ease').
* This is not the time to tell your own grief story. Keep the correspondence focused on your loved one.
* This *is* the time to be personal in your writing. Just a few thoughtfully chosen words can mean a lot.
* Borrow from your loved one's favourite song lyrics, or any other source of inspiration you know they will appreciate.
* A lovely handmade card shows a level of thoughtfulness and makes a precious keepsake if your loved one wishes.
* You could include pressed flowers or leaves in the card, or even pressed rosemary for remembrance.
* Mailing a care package (see Chapter 4) is also a lovely idea. Handmade shortbread and packaged tea could come in handy as the recipient may find themselves with more visitors than usual.

*The friend who can be silent with us in a moment of despair or confusion, who can stay with us in an hour of grief and bereavement, who can tolerate not knowing ... not healing, not curing ... that is a friend who cares.*

Henri Nouwen

## PETS

Saying farewell to a furry or feathered friend
can be difficult and traumatic, too. With more
people living alone these days, a pet as close
friend and companion can be one of the most
important relationships a person has. Thoughtful
snail mail to honour the pet's life will go a
long way to show your loved oned you care
about them.

BUTTON'S
CHARM AND
SWAGGER
WILL BE
GREATLY
MISSED

Hand-
stitch your
envelope

Our perfect companions never
have fewer than four feet.
Colette

You know what I like most
about people? Pets.
Jarod Kintz

I tell you, that dragon's the
most horrible animal I've ever
met, but the way Hagrid goes
on about it, you'd think it was
a fluffy little bunny rabbit.
J.K. Rowling, *Harry Potter* and
*the Philosopher's Stone*

Love is love, whether it goes
on two legs or four.
Gwen Cooper

I spied this cat-themed letterbox in Japan.

## WHY NOT TRY ONE OF THESE TECHNIQUES?

A cute piece of 'cat post' can be a pleasant surprise, whether you're sending it after a difficult loss or to celebrate a new arrival.

RIP dear Humphrey

Niina added bow ties

Catherine used mixed media

Marcus has been collaged

Muppet dressed as a wizard

Kat made a cat-snail

Stephanie painted watercolours

A letter to a grieving loved one doesn't have to be long, but it should be thoughtful.

Show your loved one how much you care through your words and through your presentation.

Pressed flowers (page 172) are a beautiful inclusion to a condolence letter.

Jonquils and poppies are ideal, as they have traditionally been used to express sympathy.

Homemade paper (page 78) adds a personal touch to your correspondence.

You can press whole seeds into your homemade paper to signify new life and hope.

Seeded paper can be planted in the ground to grow new things.

If a grieving loved one reaches out to you, make time for them.

Sometimes the most valuable thing you can offer is a sympathetic ear.

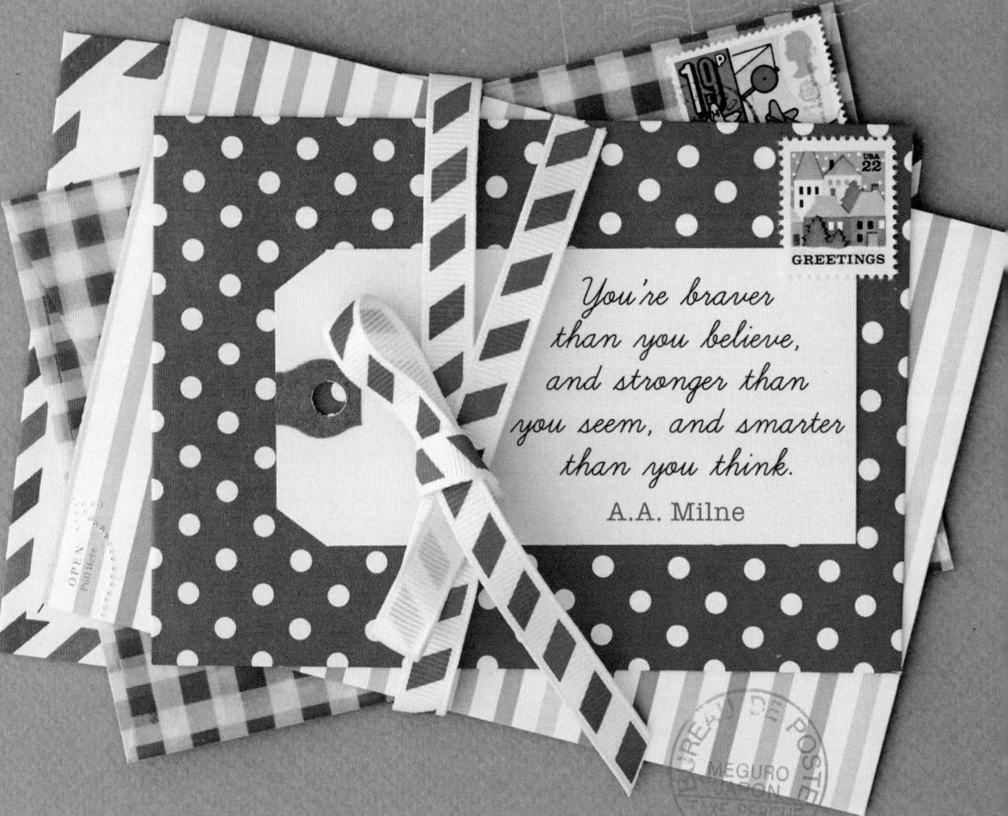
19p
USA 22
GREETINGS
You're braver
than you believe,
and stronger than
you seem, and smarter
than you think.
A.A. Milne
OPEN
Pull Here
BUREAU DE POSTE
MEGURO
JAPON
TAXE PERÇUE
YEN

## TOUGH TIMES: WHEN THINGS AREN'T QUITE AS THEY SHOULD BE

When something significant in your friend's life, like a job or a relationship, has faltered, a note in the mail is a lovely way to cheer them up and let them know you support them and are thinking of them. A tricky or clever envelope is a nice way to make the letter look interesting. You don't need to say much: the cute and colourful package will do most of the talking for you.

### Illness

When a friend is ill or recovering from an accident, things can get pretty lonely. Snail mail is the perfect thing to brighten up their day, and you should take care to really pretty up your correspondence and make something that takes time to read or unravel. After all, time is one of those things you find yourself with a lot of when you are sick!

When you're writing to a sick friend, make sure to keep your correspondence positive and focused on happy things. Take the opportunity to inject humour into your letter and make them smile or laugh. If you're not sure what to say or what the prognosis is, keep it short and heartfelt.

Another lovely thing to do is mail a care package (see Chapter 4). If your friend can't get out of the house (or hospital), they may be really missing certain foods, music, TV programs or other entertainment. Books and music, tucked up with food and anything else you know they will enjoy, will be much appreciated.

### If you are sick

If you're in hospital or convalescing at home, chances are you have a lot of time on your hands. If you are well enough to write letters, it's a lovely way to pass the long hours in each day. It also gives you the opportunity to really think about who you'd like to write to and why. Perhaps you'd like to reconnect with an old friend you've fallen out of touch with. Or, write a letter to your nearest and dearest. A letter to someone you live with can also be a lovely and unexpected gesture.

why send
flowers
when you
can send
a forest

All occasions deserve thoughtful correspondence

Make some time on the weekend to create a masterpiece

Check out Pinterest for inspiration

thank-you letters

Make a trip to your local art shop and be inspired

66 Try out an unexpected colour scheme or two ⟫→

Start a letter-writing group | No reason is ever too small

Try at least one new technique | 99 | Have fun creating

# WHEN TO WRITE: JUST BECAUSE

Do we really need an occasion to send a letter? Whether it's a card to show someone you appreciated something they did, a pretty note to say 'hello!', a letter to your future self or a message to Santa or the Easter Bunny, sometimes it's just lovely to send something *just because*.

## THANK YOU LETTERS

As our lives get busier, we often forget how to take time out and make our loved ones feel special. Saying thank you, whether it's by post or in person, is always the right thing to do, and is always appreciated. A thank you letter or card goes a long way, and can be sent for any occasion.

It could be a good time to try out that calligraphy pen you have lying around, or to use that pretty paper you've had stashed in your drawer. Words count in this kind of letter: you don't have to use many of them, but they do need to be sincere. A warning, though: sending thank you cards is addictive, and you'll find more occasions to send them than you thought possible.

message in a BOTTLE

Open me in 10 years

## 'TIME CAPSULE' LETTERS

Writing a letter to your future self – or your child or friend's future self – is a fun project to do on a spare afternoon or a rainy day.

If you're doing this project with children, encourage them to fill a container with items they will get a kick out of seeing in the future. Make sure they are things that won't be missed, though; a time capsule is not the place for a favourite toy!

Fun things to include in a time capsule
* newspaper clippings
* packaging (sweets, toys, technology, etc.)
* business cards, birthday cards, letters, yearbooks
* a CD or USB stick with your favourite music
* a completed diary or notebook
* photographs and drawings

Things to ask your future self
* What is your life like now?
* Where are you living?
* What is your job, or what are you studying? Did you end up studying _____ or doing _____?
* Are you still friends with so-and-so?
* Did you take that amazing holiday you always planned on taking?
* What is the future like?

Things to show and tell your future self about the past
* your favourite music, books and films
* what you and your friends look like
* your current goals and ambitions
* a list of the most important people and things in your life
* what your life is currently like, and how you feel about it
* your hopes and predictions for the future

DEAR EASTER BUNNY
I Hope You can make
it to ~~New~~ AustraliA.
I hope You have A safe
Trip. An have A great
time delivering eggs.
From Ari

Ari wrote a letter to the Easter Bunny

Sofia wrote a letter to the Tooth Fairy

Dear Toothfairy,
I know that people
think I am to old.
But you are never
too old for beleive.
~~But~~ So I just shake
it off ~~and~~ and continue
my day as usual.
I guess my beleif
has never dissapeared,
because beleif is a
personal thing,
It cant be, it sho-
uldnt be changed
by others.
~Sofia ♥

## LETTERS TO SANTA, THE EASTER BUNNY AND THE TOOTH FAIRY

Letters to (spoiler alert!) mythical beings provide a wonderful, creative way for children to express themselves. Encourage your children to think outside the box here!

Writing to so-called legendary figures presents a brilliant opportunity to go all-out when decorating the envelope and letter. Take your child to the post office and help them choose a special stamp. The letter-writer could draw their house, suburb or country, so their special delivery doesn't get lost, or else they might prefer to include a drawing of the North Pole, rabbit hole or fairy forest.

### When writing to Santa Claus/Father Christmas

* Ask your child to include present requests for other members of the family, including pets.
* Ask your child to include a present request for someone less fortunate than themselves.
* Encourage your child to ask Santa a question or two! You never really know – he might reply …

### When writing to the Easter Bunny

* Don't worry that children might not normally write letters to the Easter Bunny! Instead, think of all the *Alice in Wonderland*–style drawing opportunities that await if they take up this challenge.
* Ask your child to imagine they are their favourite animal, and help them write to the Easter Bunny from their chosen animal's perspective.

### When writing to the Tooth Fairy

* Encourage your child to tell the Tooth Fairy how the tooth was lost.
* Ask your child to draw their smiling face *sans* tooth, or to illustrate the losing of the tooth.

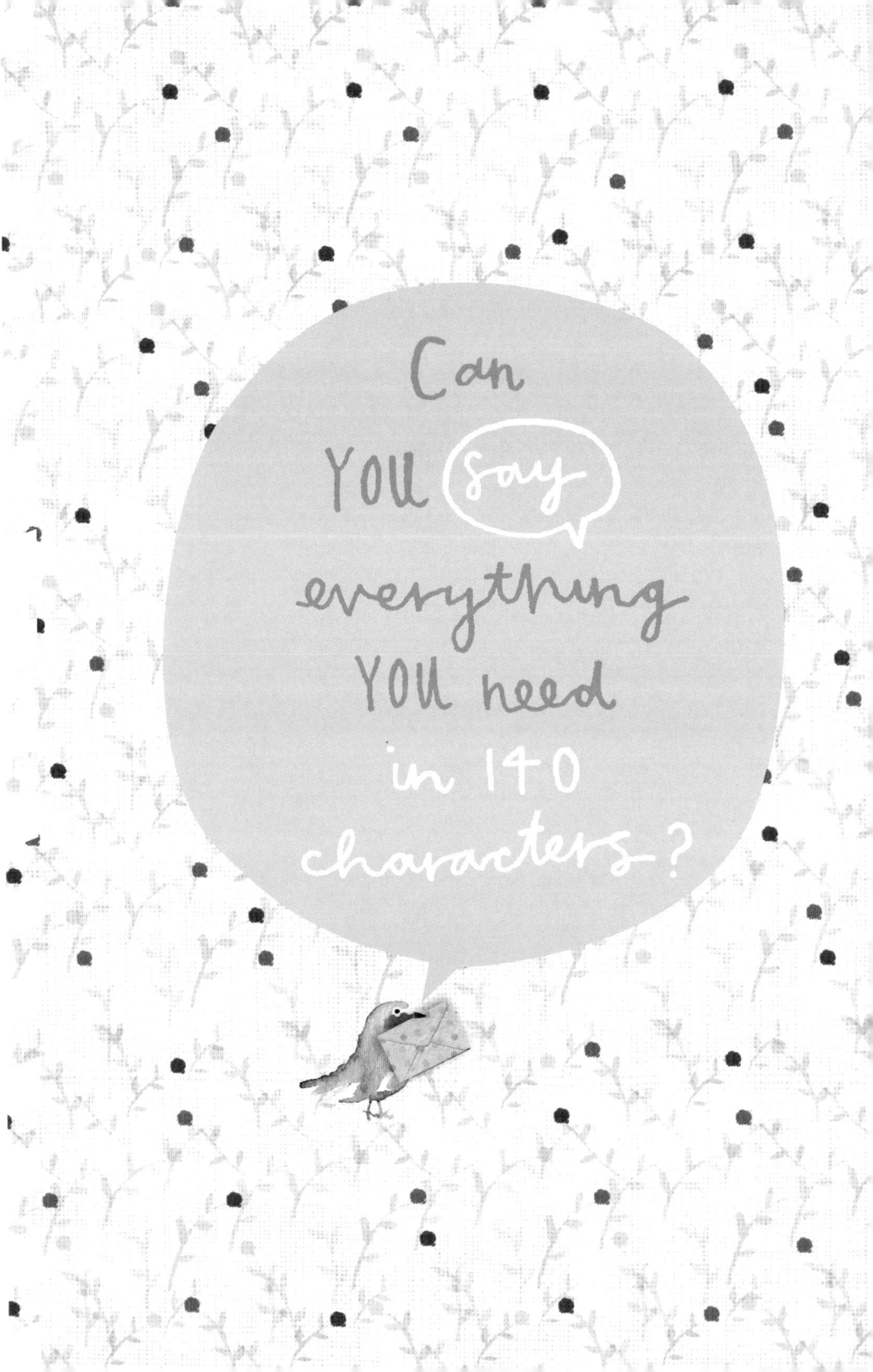
Can YOU say everything YOU need in 140 characters?

# LANGUAGE AND GRAMMAR

So you're not in a hurry, and quite frankly the language you use on social media isn't going to cut it, so keep your LOLs for other communication opportunities. It's time to use a few beautiful or well-chosen words and make a bit of a project out of your correspondence.

If you're in the mood to write like Heathcliff and Cathy, go ahead and borrow lyrics from The Smiths – though this may only be effective if you're on a windswept moor. Really, all you need to do is try and put some thoughtful and considered words together, and your intended will appreciate it – and you'll enjoy doing it. Make sure your spelling and grammar are perfect, and that you spend a bit of time practising your best handwriting. That being said, charming coffee stains on the finished product are allowed (and perhaps even encouraged).

## A FEW LANGUAGE TIPS

* Spend some time thinking about how you're feeling and why you're writing.
* Write a draft first. Leave it for a day or so, then go back and re-read it carefully. A bit of space will give you the insight needed to make your letter perfect.
* Avoid clichés and generic language.
* Don't cut corners: shun internet abbreviations and spell out what you mean.
* If your recipient is into puzzles, add a few tricky touches. Only they will know how to decipher them.
* Your letter should sound like you, but that doesn't mean you can't inject some unexpected touches. If you need help, borrow from song lyrics, poetry, your favourite films, or classic literature.

## SIGNING ON
## AND
## SIGNING OFF

There are so many salutations and valedictions to choose from and just as many ways to interpret them. How you start and end a letter is as important as what you're actually saying (or, for that matter, not saying). I have included some examples in the coming pages, sorted into categories, although it's apparently questionable to use 'dear' unless you know someone well (I am not sure when this happened, or why).

Angst and over-analysis can arise when we expect a particular tone from a correspondent but don't get it, or if the way someone signs off their letters changes suddenly. What happens when 'love' becomes 'from' (or vice versa)? If you have any difficulty deciphering your letter and are worried about the relationship, you should discuss these things in person.

## SALUTATIONS

First impressions count ... choose wisely.

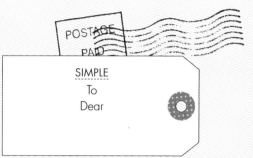

### SIMPLE
To
Dear

### FRIENDLY
Hello
Hi

### FORMAL
Dear Sir/Madam

### STERN
*The recipient's name
with nothing preceding it*

### FLOWERY
Dearest/Darling
To my dearest darling/
My dear/My darling/
To my one and only

## VALEDICTIONS

In some ways, I think it is easier to sign on than off.

It can be difficult to figure out how formally or casually you should close your letter.

### SIMPLE
From
Thank you
Thanks

### FRIENDLY
Cheers
Best
Love from
From your friend

### BUSINESS
Regards/Kind regards
Best wishes

### FORMAL
From your colleague
Yours faithfully
Yours truly
Yours sincerely

**STERN**
*The writer's name with nothing preceding it*

**FLOWERY**
Lots of love
Forever yours
*Anything ending with kisses*

**INTENSELY FLOWERY**
Forever in your debt

Your humble servant
*(although you may come off sounding like you're writing to Lord Voldemort)*

**FANTASY ROMANCE, GAME OF THRONES AND PRINCESS BRIDE-STYLE**

Moon of my life
Your sun and stars
As you wish

**PHRASES BANNED BY THIS AUTHOR**
Later
See you around

Wassup *(or any other incorrectly spelled and ugly words)*

# TERMS OF ENDEARMENT FOR YOUR SWEETHEART

**FLOWERS**
Sweet-pea
Rose
Darling bud
Petal
Blossom
Buttercup

**FOOD**
Honeybun
Sweetie-pie
Sweetie
Honey
Pancake
Pumpkin pie
Puddin'
Sugar

**TUDOR**
Dear-heart
Mine own sweetheart
Turtle dove
My dove

Get inspired and switch centuries or decades

**SHAKESPEAREAN**
Lambkin
Ladybird
Mouse
Darling bud
Duck

**VICTORIAN**
Dear miss/mister
My beloved
My dearest intimate friend

**20s**
Doll
My gal
Fly boy *(glamorous term for an aviator)*
Humdinger
Bunny
Dish

Theme your stationery up to the decade that inspires you

### 50s
**Ratpack**
Ring-a-ding-ding
Doll/Dolly bird

**Rocker**
Dreamboat
Earth angel

### 60s
**Mod/Pop**
Birdie
Babe/Baby
Sugar/Honey
Pet
Pussycat

### 70s
**Hippie**
Cat/Chick
**Rock/Glam**
Baby
Honey

### 80s
Lady
Lover

**Funk**
Hot mama

**John Hughes**
Bo hunk
Hot stuff

**Alternative**
Sweetness
My dear

### 90s
**Alternative**
Kool thing (Sonic Youth)
Boy/Girl

***Four Weddings
and a Funeral***
Lovely

***Clueless***
Betty

### 00s
**Lady** (resurrected
from the 70s and 80s)
A mashup of
everything from the
50s to the 90s

PAGE 73

## CONVERT YOUR TEXT-SPEAK TO SNAIL MAIL–FRIENDLY LANGUAGE

**GR8**
Great, brilliant, fantastic, wonderful

**IC**
I see

**GTG**
I have got to go now

**HAND**
Have a nice day

**IDGI**
I'm afraid I don't understand

**J/K**
I'm just having a joke with you

**PLS**
Please

**YW**
You are very welcome

**TMI**
This is too much information

**RUOK**
(Person's name), are you feeling alright?

**LOL**
That is really funny
I really laughed a lot

**BF**
Closest confidant

**BFF**
You will always be my closest friend

**CU**
Goodbye
**CYA**
Goodbye, farewell

**L8R/CUL8R**
I will see you later

**FOAF**
A friend of a close friend

**EZ**
A simple task
**F2F**
In person

**ASL**
How old are you, are you male or female, where are you?

**GF**
Girlfriend
**OLL**
We met online and are in love

**GU**
We live too far away from each other to make this work

LOL
Sir, your
witticisms had me
in uproarious
laughter

M8
My dear,
dear friend

WTF
I can scarcely
believe
my ears

GR8
Most excellent,
sir

GTFO
Sir, please leave
immediately
or else
reinforcements
will be on the
way

Now that you have an idea of when and what to write, you'll need something to write on. Of course, plain white paper and business envelopes will suffice, but if you're writing something personal and heartfelt, you want the whole package to match your sentiments. But beware – handmade paper and envelopes are so pretty you might not want to post them.

# 2.
# Crafting
# a letter

MAKE ME!

Handmade
paper

If you have an afternoon free, why not make your own paper? It's a wonderful way to personalise your post, and is endlessly customisable. You can decorate your paper with stamps, pressed flowers, confetti or gold sparkles, or make paper laced with seeds, so the recipient of your letter can plant it in the garden. Wherever your creativity leads you, this is a perfect project to get your snail mail looking like no-one else's. You'll never buy paper from the store again!

## YOU WILL NEED

* **2 x picture frames**
  Choose frames that are the size you want your paper to be – just make sure that the frames are the same size and can sit together.
* **Flyscreen mesh**
  You can buy this at any hardware store.
* **Tacks or staples, and waterproof duct tape**
* **A blender**
  If you plan on making a lot of paper, buy a used blender. Making paper won't break your good blender, but it can get messy … paper plus water equals gluey goo!

* **Microfibre cloths or tea towels, sponges and newspaper**
* **Scrap paper**
  You can literally use any paper, depending on what effect you want.
* **A tray**
  This can be an old cat litter tray (preferably one that Whiskers isn't using). You can even use the sink or a plastic out-tray as long as your frame can fit and be submerged in it.

## SCRAP PAPERS YOU CAN USE

* newspaper
* cards
* catalogues
* paper bags
* egg cartons
* tissue paper
* magazines
* non-waxy cardboard
* old book pages

## OPTIONAL EXTRAS

* stamps
* seeds
* flower petals
* confetti
* gold or silver sparkles
* anything else pretty!

If you'd like to stitch your paper like the example shown, you'll need a sewing machine

## 1.

**MAKING YOUR FRAME**

Remove the glass and backing from one frame and cut a piece of mesh a little larger than the entire frame. This will ensure you have enough mesh to stretch and fasten over the opening.

## 2.

Stretch the mesh over the frame and fasten it with tacks or staples. Ensure it is stretched tight across the opening. Cover the edges of the mesh with duct tape, taking care not to let the tape overlap the opening.

## 3.

Remove the glass and backing from the remaining frame. Place the flat back of the frame flush against the mesh side of the other frame, as if making a mesh sandwich. Tape the frames together securely, but don't go overboard; you will need to be able to remove the tape.

## 4.

**MAKING YOUR PAP**

Tear up the scrap paper and place in the blender with enough water to cover completely. You can add extras at this point. For a flecked look, try kitchen spices, herbs, grass or flower petals. Don't add extras that you want to remain whole, like pressed flowers or leaf skeletons. These will be added later.

**5.**

Blend the paper and water mixture. You can blend for a short time for chunkier paper, or for a longer time for a finer paper grain. Feel free to experiment!

Fill the tray with enough water to submerge the frame fully. Pour the blended paper pulp into the tray and mix to disperse it evenly in the water.

**6.**

**7.**

**8.**

Make sure that the meshless side of the frame is on top. Lower the frame into the water with a side-to-side motion, as if you are panning for gold, until the mesh is covered with pulp. Gently shake the frame from side to side in the water to even the surface out. The meshless side of the frame will keep the pulp in place.

Lift the frame from the water, making sure the pulp side is facing up. Let the excess water drain through the frame before removing the meshless side of the frame.

Place the frame, pulp side up, on microfibre towels or tea towels (anything absorbent will do, really) to drain for half an hour. At this point, you can add any reserved 'whole' extras. Try gently pushing on some pressed flowers or leaf skeletons – whatever takes your fancy.

Place the frame, pulp side down, on some newspaper. Dab a sponge on the back of the mesh to soak up any excess water. Allow to dry on the newspaper for an hour or so.

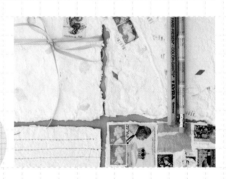

Carefully lift the frame and slowly peel off the pulp, which should now resemble a wet sheet of paper. Be very gentle, as it can tear at this stage. Once the sheet of paper is free, leave it to dry on newspaper overnight.

Voilà! You have your very own handmade paper, which will make your letters to others just that little bit more special!

Tip:
If the paper is buckled, place it under some heavy books once it is dry.

**MAKE ME!**

Upcycled
envelopes

AIR MAIL
PAR AVION

With a little ingenuity and inspiration, you can make upcycled envelopes for any occasion. Recycle the interesting scraps of paper you can't bear to part with, or, if you're looking for something special, hit up the bargain book tables at your local op shop or vintage book store and buy a title you think would work well remade into envelopes. Children's party envelopes made out of old picture books, love letters out of an old poetry tome: you get the idea.

## MAKE YOUR ENVELOPES OUT OF

* catalogues
* newspapers
* sheet music
* graph paper
* old books

* shopping bags
* lunch bags
* paper doilies
* maps
* comics

* band/event flyers
* boarding passes
* vintage kids' books
* … or a mashup of any
  of the above!

Using one of the templates provided on pages 214, 217 or 221, carefully cut out your envelope from your chosen material. Templates can easily be resized with a photocopier's enlarge/reduce function.

Use a glue stick to stick together the envelope at the seams. Or, for a prettier twist, use washi tape on the outside to keep everything in place.

If you don't want to risk your envelope getting damaged in the mail, or if you want your special envelope to be a surprise, place your upcycled envelope inside a plain white envelope.

### PRETTYING UP A STOCK-STANDARD ENVELOPE AND OTHER IDEAS
If you don't have the time to construct an envelope from scratch, try adding extras onto a regular envelope. Glue a lovely piece of paper onto the envelope's flap and trim the excess so that it sits flush. All of a sudden, your plain envelope looks just that little bit prettier!

You can also use paper bags as envelopes; you can find some lovely ones in craft stores and online, designed for parties and the like. Cut out an appropriately sized envelope flap from an eye-catching piece of paper and glue it to the bag. Or you can simply seal your letter inside the bag with washi tape.

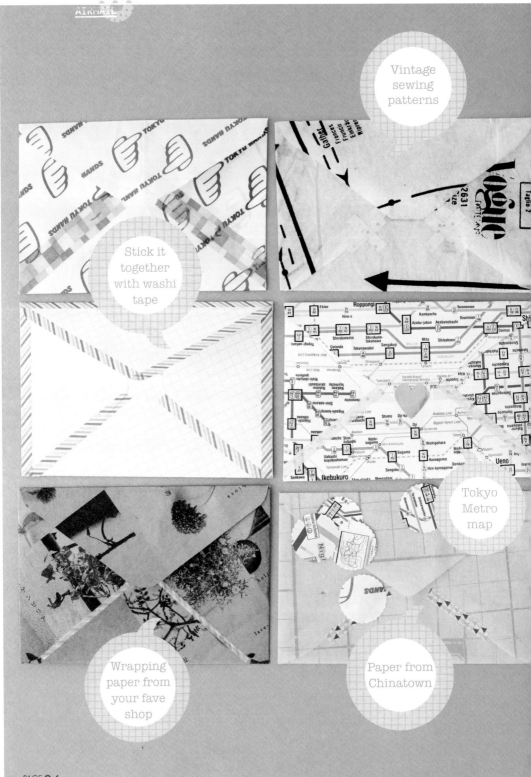

Vintage sewing patterns

Stick it together with washi tape

Tokyo Metro map

Wrapping paper from your fave shop

Paper from Chinatown

Next time you receive a bill, make sure you open it carefully, then turn it inside out! Seal with washi tape and decorate with vintage stamps and other cute things.

Bills are beautiful on the inside

Write the address here!

Fill with confetti

PAGE 87

MAKE ME!

Fabric
envelope

I love making fabric envelopes. Not only are they the perfect place to store your own snail mail, they are also a wonderful thing to send to a friend. I suggest making two of them, because when you see the final result, you'll be glad you have one of your own to keep.

YOU WILL NEED

* **An envelope**
  This will give you a template to cut your envelope from. You can also use the template on page 220.
* **2 pieces of fabric**
  These will form the inside and outside of your envelope. I used calico for the inside of my envelope and a cotton fabric for the outside.

* **Iron-on adhesive**
  You can find this at craft or sewing stores.
* **Scissors, pins, needle and thread**
* **2 buttons**
  Wooden or vintage ones are lovely!
* **Twine**

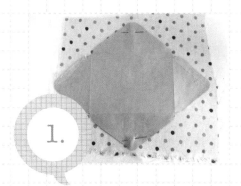

1.

Carefully take apart the envelope, or cut out your template, if using. Pin the fabric pieces and iron-on adhesive to one another and cut to the rough size of the deconstructed envelope or template. Unpin.

2.

Set aside the envelope or template. Place the inner fabric, right side down, on an ironing board.

**3.**

Place the iron-on adhesive on top of this, followed by the outer fabric, right side up. Follow the instructions for your iron-on adhesive to fuse the materials together.

Once the fabric is cool, pin the envelope or template to it and carefully cut out the shape. Iron the top, bottom and side flaps inward; the fabric should now resemble an envelope.

**4.**

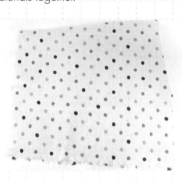

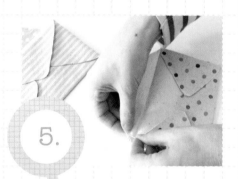

**5.**

**6.**

Hand- or machine-stitch around the edges of each flap.

Attach a button to the top flap of your envelope and one to the bottom flap. Wind some lovely twine around both buttons for a cute locking mechanism.

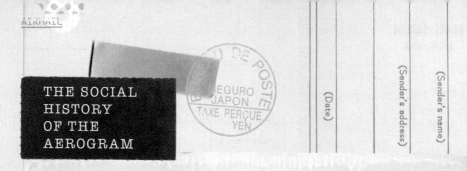

## THE SOCIAL HISTORY OF THE AEROGRAM

The aerogram's romantic reputation is very well earned. He's bilingual and well dressed; he looks expensive but is not wasteful. He whispers the languages of faraway places, and slides casually into almost any situation. He opens up easily and reveals a complex personality. He's mysterious; he's alluring; he's the aerogram.

DO NOT WRITE HERE

Aerograms are made of feather-light paper and are an all-in-one write, address, fold and self-seal snail mail solution. They were traditionally used to send letters abroad, their lightweight nature making them inexpensive to post, and their fold-up all-in-one design making them easy to use. Most aerograms came with their stamps already printed on them, so people knew the letter price before sending. Popularised during the Second World War, at a time when receiving letters was often literally the difference between life and death, the aerogram has earnt its place in history as one of the most highly sought-after and romantic forms of communication.

In the following pages you'll find some cute ideas (and updates!) that use the classically clever cut-out as a springboard. Long live the aerogram!

No.

(CENSOR'S STAMP)

Print the complete address in plain block letters in the space provided. Use typewriter, dark ink, or pencil. Write plainly. Very small writing is not suitable.

(Sender's name)

(Sender's address)

(Date)

SEE TEMPLATE PAGE 214

Perfect for
a cat-loving
friend

Seal shut
with a cute
sticker

I stitched
the flaps
instead of
gluing them

'Neko'
means
'cat' in
Japanese

Perfect
for
invitations

Tuck in his tail
and ears, then
fold him up

SEE TEMPLATE PAGES 218–219

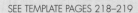

SNAIL
MAIL

# FOLD-AND-GLUE
## AEROGRAM

## PATTERNS TO TRY

XXXXXXXXXXXXXX
CROSS-STITCH

//////////////////
THICKS AND THINS

\\\\\\\\\\\\\\\\\\\\
HIGHS AND LOWS

SEE TEMPLATE PAGE 217

Go old-school with your paper choice

By air mail
Par avion

By air mail
Par avion

Try scrunching your paper

GLUE THE FLAPS ON THE INSIDE, OR
WASHI TAPE THEM ON THE OUTSIDE

SEAL THE ENVELOPE FLAP WITH WAX,
A STICKER OR WITH WASHI TAPE

Get to know the postman. He's part of your community!

It seems we all have keyboards within arm's reach these days, and it's safe to say that our handwriting has suffered! Gone are the days of immaculate script – but also, thankfully, gone are the days of smeared ink all over your hard work. Handwriting today is all about working with what you have, and I am in favour of celebrating your own hand's quirks. If you're not comfortable handwriting your letters, however, fret not: I have solutions for you, too.

# 3.
## Creative
## characters

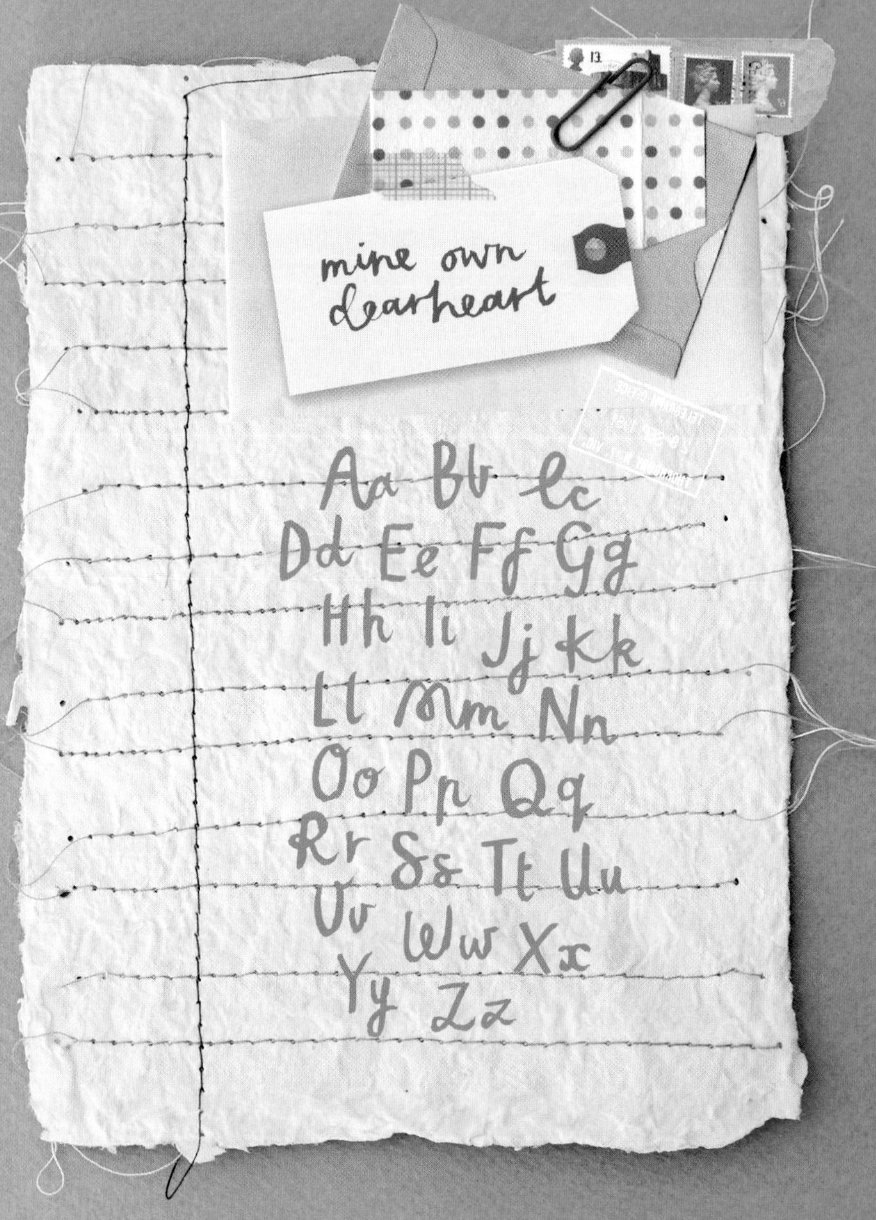

mine own
dearheart

Aa Bb Cc
Dd Ee Ff Gg
Hh Ii Jj Kk
Ll Mm Nn
Oo Pp Qq
Rr Ss Tt Uu
Uv Ww Xx
Yy Zz

## DRESS UP YOUR WORDS IN THE PRETTIEST HANDWRITING YOU CAN MUSTER

The wonderful thing about handwriting is that it is yours alone. It doesn't need to be perfect, but it can be perfected!

As a young girl, I was told by one of my primary school teachers that left-handers never have the best handwriting: it's always awkward and smudged. This was pretty upsetting information for ten-year-old me, and I was determined to try to write beautifully and prove everyone wrong.

I'm not sure anyone would call my handwriting beautiful, but I've tried to make it as good as it can possibly be. I love the wonky bits, and if I start to write uphill or down, I just incorporate it into the rest of what I'm writing. When I design books, one of my favourite things to do is to handwrite the cover type. In my view, no typeface can ever compete.

AIRMAIL

Emma Jay
P.O. box 26
Carlton north

Sharny
Yoko PLEASE KINDLY DELIVER TO:
PO BOX 26
North Carlton
Victoria · 3054
AUSTRALIA

TO:
Deb Bo...
P.O. BOX 26
CARLTON NTH
VIC. 3054

NEW YORK NY
SEP 2014 PM 4 L

AKIRA BELLI
PO BOX 26
NORTH CARLTON
VICTORIA 3054
· AUSTRALIA ·

Amanda Paino
PO Box 26
North Carlton
Victoria 3054
Australia

Amy DEVEREUX
POST OFFICE BOX

BLANKGOODS
>>> → PO BOX 26 ← <<<
CARLTON NORTH
victoria 3054

Jesse-Bree
Po Box 26
NORTH CARLTON
3054 VIC

Renee Davey
P.O. BOX 26
CARLTON
NORTH
Victoria 3054

Michelle Mackin
PO BOX 26
Carlton North

SNAIL MAIL ALL THE WAY. GIVE ME A HAN

Peader Thomas
P.O Box 26
carlton north
VIC 3054

AUSTRALIA 70c
AUSTRALIA 70c

Tijana Bozic

SHERIDAN FORDE

PLEASE DELIVER TO:
MEG SALTER
PO BOX 26
NORTH CARLTON
VICTORIA
3054

SNAIL MAIL

PAGE 105

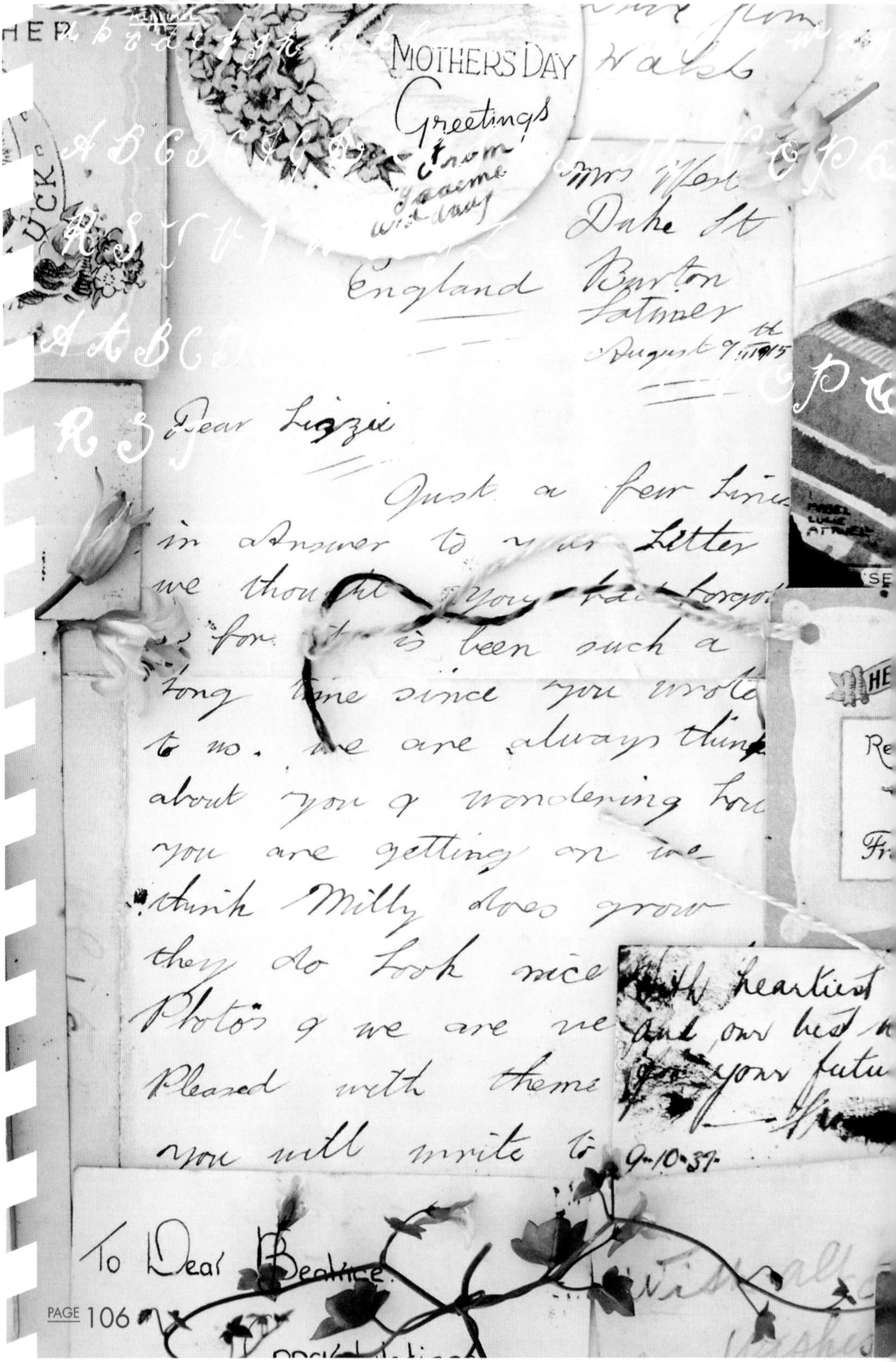

MOTHERS DAY
Greetings
From
Graeme
and Navy

Mrs West
Duke St
Burton
Latimer
England

August 7 th 15

Dear Lizzie

Just a few lines
in Answer to your Letter
we thought you had forgot
us for it is been such a
long time since you wrote
to us. we are always thinking
about you & wondering how
you are getting on we
think Milly does grow
they do look nice
Photos & we are ver
Pleased with them
you will write to

ly heartiest
and our best w
your futu

9-10-37.

To Dear Beatrice

# DON'T CHANGE YOUR STYLE, PERFECT IT!

Celebrate what makes your handwriting unique. It doesn't have to be immaculate calligraphy, or even cursive, and the quirks of your handwriting make it all the more recognisable and instantly charming.

## WHAT ARE YOUR HANDWRITING QUIRKS? DO YOU ...

* write uphill or downhill?
* loop your 'l's?
* write in all uppercase or all lowercase?
* love exclamation marks?
* do any or all of the above?

## MAKE SURE TO TRY ...

* practising your handwriting! The more you write, the more comfortable you will feel with your own style, and the more you will appreciate it.
* writing in different coloured pens and inks. White ink on natural paper is always beautiful.
* switching it up between cursive and printing. One style might suit your handwriting more than the other.
* experimenting with fat pens and skinny pens. Find the right weight for you.

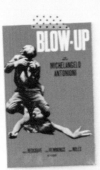

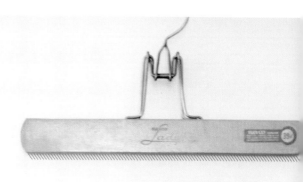

Aa Bb Cc Dd Ee Ff Gg
Hh Ii Jj Kk Ll Mm Nn
Oo Pp Qq Rr Ss Tt Uu
Vv Ww Xx Yy Zz

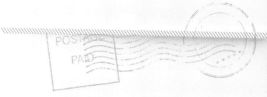

## PEN AND PAPER NOT YOUR TYPE?

If your confidence in your handwriting is pretty low, or if you just don't feel comfortable handwriting a letter, why not buy a typewriter and make some beautiful and still very personal communication the analogue way? The pressure you put on the keys will give your typewritten letter a human touch, and don't worry about striking through that spelling mistake: it all adds up to your letter being special, and mistakes can be part of that.

A typewritten letter looks fantastic with stamps, and mixing things up with a bit of handwriting, in the form of corrections or added information, can also be really beautiful.

PAT. 636.768–716.969–723.609 & CORRESP. A 5
MADE IN BELGIUM
POSTAGE PAID
15 mm (54pt)
0.551 inch
205
AAAB
BCCDD
EEEEF
EGGHH
IIIJKKL
LMMNN
OOPP
QRRS
TTUUV
VWXYZ
ÆØ&()

There are so many ways to express yourself with type. The techniques below will inspire and delight!

Mark cut out stencils

Neryl used a stencil set

Ingrid used letraset

Stephen designed a typeface

Steve tore up magazines

Graham cut type out of a map

# MAKE ME!

## Getting the most out of your handwriting

I've always loved the idea of a completely handmade book. You can find beautiful volumes in monasteries, museums and libraries – the British Library has some wonderful examples, including *The Canterbury Tales* – all painstakingly lettered by hand. (I would love to see what the shelves of the Hogwarts library hold, but sadly travel to fictional places is not yet possible!) Even though it would be labour-intensive, making a book from scratch with completely handwritten text would be a dream for me. And while you might not be up for that challenge, you can always perfect your personal handwriting style.

abcdefgABCDEFG

ascending line

cap height

waist line

baseline

descending line

ABCDEFGHIJKLMNOPQRSTUVWXYZ

abcdefghijklmnopqrstuvwxy

abcdefghijklmnopqrstuvwxy

## YOU WILL NEED

* Regular white paper
* A ruler and fine felt-tip pens or a lead pencil, for ruling guidelines
* Thin, light-coloured paper (not tracing paper, as it's too thin)
* A fountain pen or a calligraphy pen and ink (art supply stores also stock a variety of pens that mimic a fountain pen)

3.

To rule your guidelines, first decide how large you would like your letters to be. Then, giving yourself plenty of space at the top of your regular white paper, rule a solid black line. This is your **baseline**, or what you will write on. Rule a thinner line above the baseline, as tall as you want the tallest part of your lettering (the ascenders, or the tall strokes on letters like d and b) to be. This is the **ascending line**.

2.

Halfway between the baseline and ascending line, draw another thin line: the **waist line**. This is how tall letters like x, a and o will be. Halfway between the waist line and the ascending line, draw a dotted line. This is the **cap height**, which dictates how tall your upper-case letters will be. (If you like, your upper-case letters and ascenders can be the same height.) Finally, rule the **descending line**, which controls how low the lowest point (or the descender) of letters like q and p is. If you're ruling a full page of guidelines, this descending line will be the ascending line of the line below.

You can always play around with the proportions of your guidelines to get different results.

Place your guideline sheet under the thin sheet of paper; the lines should show through faintly. This will allow you to write in a straight line and to make sure the proportions of your handwriting are consistent. Write out the alphabet in upper and lower cases, using your own handwriting style (see example, left). Play around with different letterforms, experimenting with the quirks of your handwriting. From here, you can switch between printing your lowercase letters and joining them up. Which do you prefer? Does your handwriting have a slant? It's fine if it does; you just need to keep it consistent. Once you're happy with your final personal style, build up muscle memory by copying out a paragraph or two from your favourite book, taking care to stick to your handwriting decisions.

*If you spend most of your day at a computer, you might find your hand gets a bit tired, but stick at it.*

*I am a big believer in the beauty of mistakes, so don't throw out any of your attempts!*

a b c d e f g h i j k l m n o
p q r s t u v w x y z

a b c d e f g h i j k l m
n o p q r s t u v w x y z

a b c d e f g h i j k l m n o
p q r s t u v w x y z

a b c d e f g h i j k l m
n o p q r s t u v w x y z

a b c d e f g h i j k l m
n o p q r s t u v w x y z

d e f g h i j k l m
q r s t u v w x y z

A letter from
Jane Austen
to her sister
Cassandra

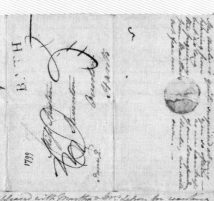

13. Queen Square - Sunday June 2.

My dear Cassandra

I am obliged to you for two letters, one from yourself & the other from Mary, for of the latter I knew nothing till on the receipt of yours yesterday, when the Pigeon Basket was examined & I received my due. As I have written to her since the time which ought to have brought me hers, I suppose she will consider herself as I desire to consider her, still in my debt. I will lay out all the little Judgement I have in endeavouring to get such stockings for Anne as she will approve; but I do not know that I shall execute Martha's commission at all, for I am not fond of ordering shoes, & at any rate they shall all have flat heels. What must I tell you of Edward? Truth or Falsehood? — I will try the former, & you may chuse for yourself another time. He was better yesterday than he had been for two or three days before, about as well as while he was at Steventon. He drinks at the Hetling Pump, is to bathe tomorrow, & try Electricity on Tuesday; he proposed the latter himself to Dr Fellowes, who made no objection to it, but I fancy we are all unanimous in expecting no advantage from it. At present I have no great notion of our staying here beyond the Month. I heard from Charles last week; they were to sail on Wednesday. My Mother seems remarkably well. My Uncle overwalked himself at first

It is. — I spent friday evening with the Mapletons, & was obliged to submit to being pleased inspite of my inclination. We took a very charming walk from 6 to 8 up Beacon Hill & across some fields to the Village of Charlcombe, which is sweetly situated in a little green Valley, as a village with such a name ought to be. Marianne is sensible & intelligent, & even Jane considering how fair she is, is not unpleasing. We had a Miss North & a Mr Gould of our party; the latter walked home with me after Tea; he is a very young Man, just entered of Oxford, wears spectacles, & has heard that Evelina was written by Dr Johnson. I am afraid I cannot undertake to carry Martha's shoes home, for tho' we had plenty of room in our Trunks when we came, we shall have many more things to take back, & I must allow besides for my packing. There is to be a grand gala on tuesday evening in Sydney Gardens; a Concert, with Illuminations & fireworks; to the latter Eliz: & I look forward with pleasure, & even the Concert will have more than its usual charm with me, as the gardens are large enough for me to get pretty well beyond the reach of its sound. In the morning Lady Willoughby is to present the Colours to some Corps of Yeomanry or other, in the Crescent — & that such festivities may have a proper commencement, we think of going to

quite pleased with Martha & Mrs Lefroy for wanting the pattern of our Caps, but I am not so well pleased with your giving it to them. Some wish, some prevailing wish always to the annexation of everybody's Mind, & in going thro' this, you leave them to form some other which will probably be half so innocent. — I shall not be sorry to Frank. Duty & Love &c.

Yours affecly Jane.

now only treats in in Cas, but is otherwise very. My Cloak is come home, & here follows the pattern of lace. If you do not think it wide enough, I can give 3 or 4 more for yours, & not go beyond the two Guineas, for my Cloak altogether does not cost quite two pounds. — I like it very much, & can now exclaim with delight, like J. Bond at Hay-Harvest, "This is what I have been looking for these three years." I saw some gauzes in a shop in Bath Street yesterday at only 4 a yard, but they were not so good or so pretty as mine. Flowers are very much worn, & Fruit is still more the thing. Eliz: has a bunch of Strawberries, & I have seen Grapes, Cherries, Plums & Apricots. There are likewise Almonds & raisins, french plums & apricots at the Grocers, but I have never seen any of them in hats. A plum or green gage would cost three shillings; Cherries & Grapes about 5 I believe — but this is the very dearest fruit. My Aunt has told me of a shop near Walcot Church, to which I shall go in quest of something for you. I have never seen an old Woman at the Pump room. Eliz: has given me a hat, & it is not only a pretty hat, but a pretty style of hat too, something like Eliza's — only, instead of being all straw, half of it is narrow purple ribbon. I flatter myself however that you can understand very little of it, from this description. Heaven forbid that I should ever offer such encouragement to Explanations, as to give a clear one on any occasion myself. But I must write no more of this.

13 Queen Square, Sunday (June 2).

My dear Cassandra,

I am obliged to you for two letters, one from yourself and the other from Mary, for of the latter I knew nothing till on the receipt of yours yesterday, when the pigeon-basket was examined, and I received my due. As I have written to her since the time which ought to have brought me hers, I suppose she will consider herself, as I choose to consider her, still in my debt.

I will lay out all the little judgment I have in endeavoring to get such stockings for Anna as she will approve; but I do not know that I shall execute Martha's commission at all, for I am not fond of ordering shoes; and, at any rate, they shall all have flat heels.

What must I tell you of Edward? Truth or falsehood? I will try the former, and you may choose for yourself another time. He was better yesterday than he had been for two or three days before,—about as well as while he was at Steventon. He drinks at the Hetling Pump, is to bathe to-morrow, and try electricity on Tuesday. He proposed the latter himself to Dr. Fellowes, who made no objection to it, but I fancy we are all unanimous in expecting no advantage from it. At present I have no great notion of our staying here beyond the month.

I heard from Charles last week; they were to sail on Wednesday.

My mother seems remarkably well. My uncle overwalked himself at first, and can now only travel in a chair, but is otherwise very well.

My cloak is come home. I like it very much, and can now exclaim with delight, like J. Bond at hay-harvest, "This is what I have been looking for these three years." I saw some gauzes in a shop in Bath Street yesterday at only 4d. a yard, but they were not so good or so pretty as mine. Flowers are very much worn, and fruit is still more the thing. Elizabeth has a bunch of strawberries, and I have seen grapes, cherries, plums, and apricots. There are likewise almonds and raisins, French plums, and tamarinds at the grocers', but I have never seen any of them in hats. A plum or greengage would cost three shillings; cherries and grapes about five, I believe, but this is at some of the dearest shops. My aunt has told me of a very cheap one, near Walcot Church, to which I shall go in quest of something for you. I have never seen an old woman at the pump-room.

Elizabeth has given me a hat, and it is not only a pretty hat, but a pretty style of hat too. It is something like Eliza's, only, instead of being all straw, half of it is narrow purple ribbon. I flatter myself, however, that you can understand very little of it from this description. Heaven forbid that I should ever offer such encouragement to explanations as to give a clear one on any occasion myself! But I must write no more of this....

I spent Friday evening with the Mapletons, and was obliged to submit to being pleased in spite of my inclination. We took a very charming walk from six to eight up Beacon Hill, and across some fields, to the village of Charlecombe, which is sweetly situated in a little green valley, as a village with such a name ought to be. Marianne is sensible and intelligent; and even Jane, considering how fair she is, is not unpleasant. We had a Miss North and a Mr. Gould of our party; the latter walked home with me after tea. He is a very young man, just entered Oxford, wears spectacles, and has heard that "Evelina" was written by Dr. Johnson.

I am afraid I cannot undertake to carry Martha's shoes home, for, though we had plenty of room in our trunks when we came, we shall have many more things to take back, and I must allow besides for my packing.

There is to be a grand gala on Tuesday evening in Sydney Gardens, a concert, with illuminations and fireworks. To the latter Elizabeth and I look forward with pleasure, and even the concert will have more than its usual charm for me, as the gardens are large enough for me to get pretty well beyond the reach of its sound. In the morning Lady Willoughby is to present the colors to some corps, or Yeomanry, or other, in the Crescent, and that such festivities may have a proper commencement, we think of going to....

I am quite pleased with Martha and Mrs. Lefroy for wanting the pattern of our caps, but I am not so well pleased with your giving it to them. Some wish, some prevailing wish, is necessary to the animation of everybody's mind, and in gratifying this you leave them to form some other which will not probably be half so innocent. I shall not forget to write to Frank. Duty and love, etc.

Yours affectionately,
Jane.

My uncle is quite surprised at my hearing from you so often; but as long as we can keep the frequency of our correspondence from Martha's uncle, we will not fear our own.

Miss Austen, Steventon.

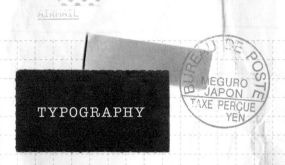

# TYPOGRAPHY

Don't despair if handwriting or old-fashioned typewriting aren't your thing. Prettying up your correspondence by way of a computer is a viable and more interesting option than you may think.

## A FEW TYPOGRAPHIC TIPS

* Do a little bit of typographic research. Do you have a favourite magazine or newspaper? Look at the fonts they use. If you have a sample, WhatTheFont (www.myfonts.com/WhatTheFont/) can help you identify it.

* Don't worry if a font you've found costs an arm and a leg. There are plenty of free font options available online – just search for 'free fonts'. Browse for something that looks similar, and download away.

* If you have a favourite decorative typeface that's a bit hard to read, try using it for the addressee's name, and set the rest of the letter in a simpler typeface.

* Good typography always has a hierarchy. If you are using headings, they need to stand out from the rest of the text. It's the perfect opportunity to use a decorative typeface – or even colour.

* Choose the right typeface for the occasion. Using a wacky font for a letter to a grieving friend is not only inappropriate, but it could also be seen as insincere or even rude.

* When approaching typography, less is more. Don't use twenty different typefaces in a letter; pick a few of your favourites and go from there.

* After typesetting your letter in your favourite font, make each paragraph a different point size. Then, print out your letter and find out which size looks best and makes for easy reading. Set your final letter in this size. You could start at 9pt and go up to 12pt; anything above 12pt, depending on the typeface, tends to be too big.

## SANS SERIF FONTS

ABCDEFGHIJKLMNOPQRSTUVWXYZ
ABCDEFGHIJKLMNOPQRSTUVWXYZ
**ABCDEFGHIJKLMNOPQRSTUVWXYZ**

FONT
BEBAS NEUE
Use for: invitations,
graphic letters

abcdefghijklmnopqrstuvwxyz
ABCDEFGHIJKLMNOPQRSTUVWXYZ
*abcdefghijklmnopqrstuvwxyz*
*ABCDEFGHIJKLMNOPQRSTUVWXYZ*
**abcdefghijklmnopqrstuvwxyz**
**ABCDEFGHIJKLMNOPQRSTUVWXYZ**
*abcdefghijklmnopqrstuvwxyz*
*ABCDEFGHIJKLMNOPQRSTUVWXYZ*
**abcdefghijklmnopqrstuvwxyz**
**ABCDEFGHIJKLMNOPQRSTUVWXYZ**

FONT
AILERON
Use for: letter text,
invitations

## SERIF FONTS

**abcdefghijklmnopqrstuvwxyz**
**ABCDEFGHIJKLMNOPQRST**
**UVWXYZ**

FONT
PISTILLI ROMAN
Use for: headings,
invitations

abcdefghijklmnopqrstuvwxyz
ABCDEFGHIJKLMNOPQRSTUVWXYZ
*abcdefghijklmnopqrstuvwxyz*
*ABCDEFGHIJKLMNOPQRSTUVWXYZ*

FONT
LORA
Use for: letter text,
headings, invitations

abcdefghijklmnopqrstuvwxyz
ABCDEFGHIJKLMNOPQRSTUVWXYZ
æfbƈɫðﬅﬆﬅﬁﬃﬄﬀﬂﬀﬂﬀﬂﬁﬁﬂﬀﬃ¼½¾⅔tt šþ✒ﬀﬁﬂžýfz
ﬀﬃﬀﬃﬀﬃﬂ ﬃﬄﬀﬃﬂﬀﬁﬂﬀ∫ΣLMNNΠ

FONT
DAY ROMAN
Use for: letter text,
headings, invitations

Day Roman has beautiful ligatures; they can beautify
the text by adding a special touch to certain letter
combinations, like 'ff', 'st' or 'ae'.

# Never
# write
# a letter
# while
# you are
# angry.

CHINESE PROVERB

...

Letters can be any size.
They can be essays
on love, politics or life,
or just a few well-
chosen words.

🕊

...

I consider it a good rule for letter-writing
to leave unmentioned what the recipient
already knows, and instead tell him
something new.

*Sigmund Freud*

*abcdefghijklmnopqrstuvwxyz*
*ABCDEFGHIJKLMNOPQ*
*RSTUVWXYZ*

**FONT
CHOPIN SCRIPT**
Use for: letter text, headings, invitations

*abcdefghijklmnopqrstuvwxyz*
*ABCDEFGHIJKLMNOPQRS*
*TUVWXYZ*

**FONT
LEARNING CURVE**
Use for: letter text, headings, invitations

*abcdefghijklmnopqrstuvwxyz*
*ABCDEFGHIJKLM*
*NOPQRSTUVWXYZ*

**FONT
BEAUTIFUL ES**
Use for: letter text, invitations

*abcdefghijklmnopqrstuvwxyz*
*ABCDEFGHIJKLM*
*NOPQRSTUVWXYZ*

**FONT
CAC CHAMPAGNE**
Use for: letter text, invitations

Type the font names into your search engine and get started!

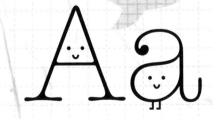

Sometimes, our loved ones just need a little more TLC. They might have a new baby, or be especially busy at work, or they could be ill or grieving. A care package – a simple, inexpensive gesture, full to the brim with small comforts – is a good way to take the pressure off your loved one just a little, and to show them you care. Today's express post options mean that even if you're across the other side of the country, you can lend a helping hand.

# 4.

# Brown paper packages tied up with string

Brown paper packages tied up with string. These are a few of my favourite things!

## CARE PACKAGES AND HOW TO PREPARE THEM

Care packages are a great example of actions speaking louder than words. Your loved one is in need of some serious TLC, and this is the perfect way to show you care.

### CARE PACKAGES ARE IDEAL FOR FRIENDS WHO ...

* have moved to another country
* have just had a baby
* have started a new job
* have lost their job
* have ended a long-term relationship
* have just moved out of home
* need cheering up
* are sick
* are grieving
* you think would love a care package, just because!

The idea behind care packages is simple: fill a box with things that are thoughtful, light to pack and perhaps a little indulgent – the kind of items your friend might be too busy or stressed out to buy for themselves.

### YOU MIGHT INCLUDE ...

* tea
* homemade biscuits
* homemade chocolates
* a good book or DVD
* something funny or witty or both
* dried flowers
* lovely soap
* a photo of you and the recipient, or any other meaningful photo
* socks (if you are a knitter, then hand-knitted socks would be amazing)
* anything else homemade (and preferably light)

Over the next few pages, you'll find some care package ideas for specific situations. But don't feel like you have to follow them to the letter: after all, you know the recipient best.

## *Making your care package special*

If you want to add an extra personal touch to your care package, why not decorate the box? Use wrapping paper, washi tape, textas or pens – whatever takes your fancy! There's no reason why you can't treat it like a letter: ask the post office for their prettiest stamps, take care with your handwriting and perhaps even use a bit of flowery language, like 'To the most amazing daughter' or 'To the wonderful (recipient's name)'.

### FOR SOMEONE LIVING OVERSEAS

* their favourite treats from home
* their favourite magazine from home
* a book from a local author, or one in their native language
* business cards and coasters from their favourite cafe, bar or restaurant
* polaroids
* freshly ground coffee

### FOR SOMEONE WHO HAS JUST MOVED OUT OF HOME

* chocolate
* tea or freshly ground coffee
* new pillowcases
* hand-knitted socks
* a framed photo collage

### FOR GRANDMA AND GRANDPA

* polaroids of your family
* drawings and letters
* homemade chocolates and biscuits
* reading material they might enjoy – whether it's a book, a magazine or a newspaper article you have read recently

### FOR SOMEONE WHO HAS LOST THEIR JOB OR HAS ENDED A RELATIONSHIP

* chocolate
* tea or freshly ground coffee
* movie tickets
* magazines

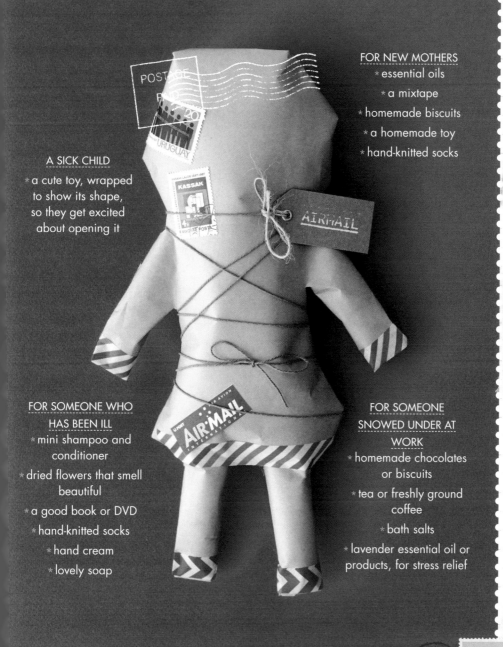

**FOR NEW MOTHERS**
* essential oils
* a mixtape
* homemade biscuits
* a homemade toy
* hand-knitted socks

**A SICK CHILD**
* a cute toy, wrapped
to show its shape,
so they get excited
about opening it

**FOR SOMEONE WHO
HAS BEEN ILL**
* mini shampoo and
conditioner
* dried flowers that smell
beautiful
* a good book or DVD
* hand-knitted socks
* hand cream
* lovely soap

**FOR SOMEONE
SNOWED UNDER AT
WORK**
* homemade chocolates
or biscuits
* tea or freshly ground
coffee
* bath salts
* lavender essential oil or
products, for stress relief

POSTAGE
PAID
URUGUAY

KASSAK

AIRMAIL

AIR·MAIL
INTERNATIONAL

Go analogue with a mix tape

Make a cloth or paper book cover

Include favourite things

Ask your post office for some airmail stickers and add them to everything!

Have fun wrapping cute things

Pretty up with vintage stamps

Cute up rice crackers

Decorate your shortbread

Include fun keepsakes from home

Homemade chocolates are always appreciated

Package with care

Try making separate batches using white, milk and dark chocolate, then package a variety.

## pretty chocolate treats

Beautifully presented chocolates are a lovely inclusion in any care package. Easy to make, they are suitable for almost any situation, and are a welcome addition to your loved one's cupboard for when unexpected guests drop by. If the recipient doesn't have a sweet tooth, they can be shared with family and friends.

Once you master chocolate decorating, you'll find it hard to resist making a batch for your next gift-giving occasion. You'll find some lovely chocolate moulds at your local culinary or craft store, or on the internet.

// Half-fill a small saucepan with water and bring to a simmer. Chop your chocolate of choice into small pieces and place in a glass bowl you have set on top of the saucepan, making sure the bottom of the bowl doesn't touch the water.

// Stir until the chocolate has melted, removing the bowl from the heat when there are still a few tiny unmelted pieces left, so the chocolate doesn't burn (the residual heat will melt these last bits).

// At this point, you can add a little neutral oil (canola or vegetable is fine) to your chocolate, about a teaspoon for a whole block, to help give the finished product a bit of shine.

// Spoon the chocolate mixture into your moulds and set in the fridge for at least 2 hours. Avoid overfilling the moulds, as this will give your treats rough edges that you will have to remove before packaging.

The ANZAC biscuit was the ultimate care package inclusion for Australian and New Zealand soldiers in the First and Second World Wars. The recipe was designed to last.

## anzac biscuits

190 g (6½ oz) plain (all-purpose) flour, sifted
90 g (3 oz) rolled oats
110 g (4 oz) caster (superfine) sugar

65 g (2¼ oz) desiccated (dried, shredded) coconut
2 tablespoons golden syrup

150 g (5½ oz) unsalted butter, chopped (see note)
½ teaspoon bicarbonate of soda (baking soda)

// Preheat the oven to 170°C (340°F).

// In a large bowl, combine the flour, oats, sugar and coconut.

// Place the golden syrup and butter in a small saucepan over a low heat and stir until melted. Remove from the heat. Mix the bicarbonate of soda with 1½ tablespoons of water and add to the golden syrup mixture. Take care, as it will bubble up while you stir.

// Pour the golden syrup mixture into the dry ingredients and stir until completely combined.

// Roll tablespoonfuls of dough into balls and place on baking trays lined with baking paper, pressing down on the tops to flatten slightly.

// Bake for 12 minutes or until golden brown. Transfer to a wire rack to cool.

Makes 24

**Note:** *If your recipient is vegan, substitute the butter with 125 ml (4 fl oz) light olive oil.*

**Variation:** *For a citrus zing, add two teaspoons of finely grated lemon zest in with the dry ingredients.*

Shortbread can last several weeks in an airtight container, so it's no problem if the mail is delayed!

## classic shortbread with pressed flowers

Pressed edible flowers, such as violets or thyme

125 g (4½ oz) unsalted butter

55 g (2 oz) caster (superfine) sugar, plus extra for sprinkling

180 g (6½ oz) plain (all-purpose) flour, or gluten-free flour of your choice

Pinch of salt

// If pressing the edible flowers yourself, you will need to do so at least a few days in advance; a week before you make the shortbread is best. I used violets and thyme.

// Preheat the oven to 190°C (375°F).

// Using an electric mixer, cream the butter and sugar until pale and fluffy. Sift the flour and salt into the same bowl and fold through the butter mixture until combined. Turn out onto a clean work surface and knead the dough until it becomes a smooth ball.

// Flatten the dough ball, then place between two sheets of baking paper and roll out to a thickness of 1 cm (½ in). Leaving the dough sandwiched between the baking paper, transfer to the refrigerator to cool for 15–20 minutes.

// Remove the top sheet of baking paper from the dough. Using a cute biscuit (cookie) cutter, cut out shapes and place them onto a baking tray lined with baking paper. Press a small flower into the top of each shortbread, then sprinkle with caster sugar. Roll the excess mixture back into a ball and repeat the process until all of the dough has been used.

// Bake for 15–20 minutes, or until pale golden brown. Transfer to a wire rack to cool.

Makes approximately 24 biscuits (depending on the size of your cutter)

Craft up
brightly
coloured
bags

Choose
a colour
theme

AIR MAIL
INTERNATIONAL

Everyone loves cute socks

Include a letter!

AIR·MAIL
INTERNATIONAL

AIR·MAIL
PAR AVION
INTERNATIONAL

Clear bags show off pretty items

SNAIL MAIL
SNAIL MAIL
SNAIL MAIL
SNAIL MAIL

You can write
your letter, seal it and
leave it at that, but you will
be missing out on some of the
best fun you can have with snail
mail (besides receiving it). Decorating
your letter and envelope to match your
personality or the occasion makes
a piece of post extra-special, and
transforms it from something
everyday into a keepsake
your recipient can
treasure forever.

# 5.
# Post with personality

PROJECTS!

Some
equipment
you may
need

paper
punches

candles

raised
buttons

needle and thread

champagne
corks

stickers

glue

B, 2B
and 4B
pencils

cutting mat

rubber
for
making
stamps

stamp
carving
tools

stamps

scissors

rulers          letter opener          calligraphy pens

buttons

sticky tape

pins

washi tape

erasers

fabric

special stamps

craft supplies

string

PVA (Elmer's)
glue

type stencil

ribbon

ink pads

coloured paper
upcycled paper
old sheet music
paper bags

flowers

## STATIONERY OBSESSION

Quite a few years ago now, while working for a lovely design studio called Marcus Livio Design, I came up with the logo for a paper company called Paperpoint. It won quite a few awards, and to this day it's one of my favourite things I've ever designed. I guess that's because I'm pretty passionate about paper and stationery! I've had my own stationery company with my friends Trisha and Olga, and have two card and notebook ranges with my publisher, Hardie Grant Books (see designs below). So I guess you could say I have OSD: obsessive stationery disorder!

I have a vast collection of stationery, mostly bought on overseas trips to Europe and Japan. I collect everything, from classic cotton-based writing sets to bright, pattern-heavy Japanese designs. But don't worry if you're not about to hop on a jet plane: you can find a huge range of beautiful stationery online, enough to start your own obsession.

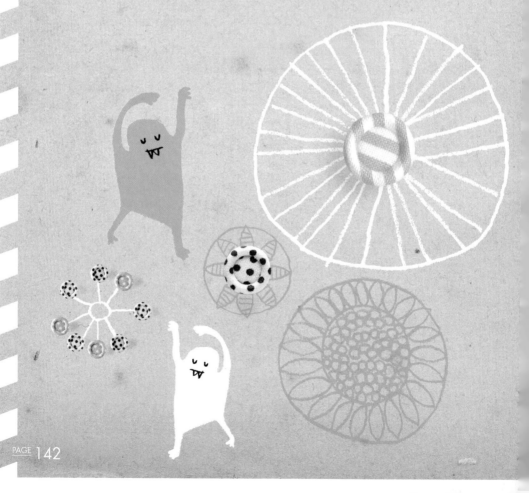

## STARTING A PAPER COLLECTION

In a way, paper often chooses you. Once you decide to get serious and start collecting, every pretty piece of wrapping paper or scrap paper, and every interesting newspaper or catalogue spread will find its way into your stockpile. They'll sit alongside graph paper and tracing pads, packets of coloured or perhaps sparkly paper, and paper with textures or patterns. Before things get out of control, you'll need to find a flat place to store your paper, keeping in mind that it will keep on growing – so think carefully about where your collection will live.

Oh, and never, ever throw out the scraps! Simply use them to beautify your more utilitarian pieces of paper: a plain base paired with a few pops of colour is a shortcut to cute stationery. And if you are stumped by where to start, try visiting your local office supply store, two-dollar shops, or your local arts and crafts suppliers.

Ideas for your collection

* graph paper
* tracing paper
* coloured paper
* cotton paper

* natural paper
* kraft paper
* patterned paper
* sparkly paper

* anything you think is pretty enough to reuse

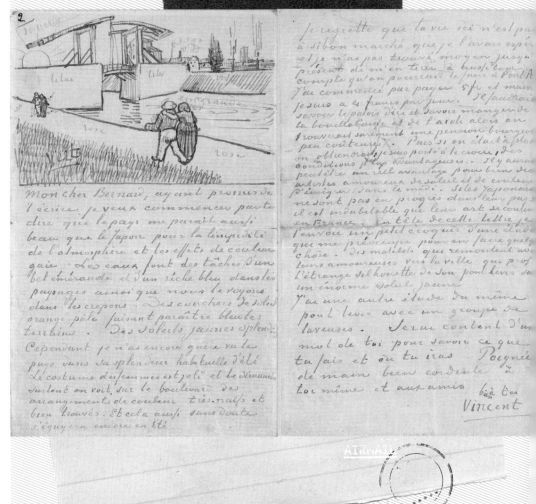

My dear Bernard,

Having promised to write to you, I want to begin by telling you that this part of the world seems to me as beautiful as Japan for the limpidity of the atmosphere and the gay colour effects. The stretches of water make patches of a beautiful emerald and a rich blue in the landscapes, as we see it in the Japanese prints. Pale orange sunsets making the fields look blue—glorious yellow suns. So far, however, I've hardly seen this part of the world in its usual summer splendour. The women's costume is pretty, and especially on the boulevard on Sunday you see some very naive and well-chosen arrangements of colour. And that, too, will doubtless get even livelier in summer.

I regret that living here isn't as cheap as I'd hoped, and until now I haven't found a way of getting by as easily as one could in Pont-Aven. I started out paying 5 francs and now I'm on 4 francs a day. One would need to know the local patois, and know how to eat bouillabaisse and aioli, then one would surely find an inexpensive family boardinghouse. Then if there were several of us, I'm inclined to believe we would get more favourable terms. Perhaps there would be a real advantage in emigrating to the south for many artists in love with sunshine and colour. The Japanese may not be making progress in their country, but there is no doubt that their art is being carried on in France. At the top of this letter I am sending you a little sketch of a study that is preoccupying me as to how to make something of it—sailors coming back with their sweethearts toward the town, which projects the strange silhouette of its drawbridge against a huge yellow sun.

I have another study of the same drawbridge with a group of washerwomen. Shall be happy to have a line from you to know what you're doing and where you're going to go. A very warm handshake to you and the friends.

Yours,
Vincent

Cut washi tape into small triangles and make a pattern

Add some stickers

Lay washi tape over grid paper and make patterns

## BRIGHTEN THINGS UP

Colour and pattern, even when used simply, can really make a difference to your mail. Don't be shy! Play around with what you have – a little colour goes a long way (but sometimes even more colour is better)!

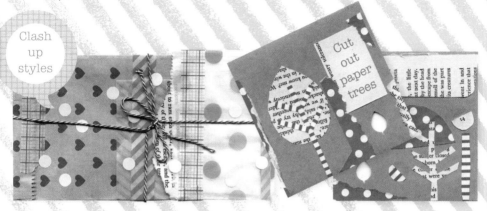

Clash up styles

Cut out paper trees

Try using one colourway and change up the patterns

Cut out clouds and rain

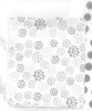

Mix spots with florals

Pop bright things in a clear envelope

Stamping onto fabric

Hand-carved stamps

# RUBBER STAMPS

Stamping a letter is an excellent way to make your correspondence beautiful and personal. You can potato stamp, carve out your own rubber stamp or easily send one off to be made. If you want to go all out, getting your own embossing seal made (see page 159) can help make your letters super beautiful. Any or all of these ideas are a great way to get crafty and have some fun making letter art.

## GETTING YOUR STAMPS PROFESSIONALLY MADE

On page 151 you'll find stamp designs you can take to a manufacturer. If you'd like fine detail in your designs, professionally made stamps are the way to go.

## CARVING A RUBBER STAMP

This is the most advanced of the stamp-making techniques. It does take a bit of practise, but when mastered, it's the most rewarding. First, you'll need to visit your art supply store to buy a carving tool set suitable for rubber. Your set should include a tool fine enough to carve detail. Buy some rubber blocks here too, or else you can carve your design into erasers. Trace or draw your design onto your piece of rubber and, with your tool nearly parallel to the rubber, start carving. Use a larger tool to carve away the excess rubber from your design, and the smaller tool to carefully carve the edges and detail. Be careful as carving tools are very sharp!

Using the eraser on the end of a pencil as a stamp
Using a scalpel, cut a design into the eraser on the end of a pencil. As the eraser is very small, simple, strong shapes like lines or a triangle work well.

Designs for all of the techniques mentioned can be found on the next two pages!

## POTATO STAMPING

Potato stamping is the simplest and cheapest way to get started on your stamping odyssey. It's also a great activity to share with children. Potato stamping works the best with a very simple and bold design. Cut a potato in half and draw your design with pencil onto the flat side. With a scalpel, first cut away the excess potato, then cut the rest of your design out. Stamp your potato half in ink and start creating.

## Stamp designs

Use the stamp designs on these pages to get started. When you're feeling confident, create your own design or modify these ones to your liking. I would recommend tracing the potato stamp designs and photocopying the hand-carved designs. If getting a stamp professionally made, send the stamp-maker a scan, or take in a photocopy. The price of having a stamp made is usually governed by size, so ask about the best size and price for you. Happy stamping!

Designs for hand-carving

1.

2.

3.

4.

For erasers on top of pencils

5.

Designs for potato stamps

Potato stamping makes fantastic wrapping paper and, if you have fabric ink, is perfect for custom textiles.

1.

2.

3.

4.

Designs for professionally made stamps

1.

2.

3.

4.

5.

6.

7.

## MAKE ME!

## Homemade
## wax seal

Next time you celebrate something special with a bottle of champagne, save the cork to make your very own wax seal. You'll also need a cute raised button, but remember, each champagne brand will have a slightly different cork, so take your cork to the button shop with you to find its perfect match.

* **A hot glue gun or superglue**
* **A metal button with a raised design**
  Buttons that come with a metal loop on the back, rather than buttonholes, are called shank buttons. Shank buttons with a design that doesn't come to too much of a point in the centre are best.

* **A wine or champagne cork**
  The flat base of the cork should be the same size as the button.
* **Sealing wax**
  This can be bought at specialty paper stores or online.
* **Paper and envelopes**
  Scrap for practising on, and the good stuff.

**1.**

Glue the back of the button to the flat base of the cork. If you find that the shank of the button is getting in the way, use a pair of jewellery pliers to carefully flatten or remove it. If using superglue, allow it to dry fully according to the manufacturer's instructions.

**2.**

A cold seal is most effective, as the wax is less likely to stick to the seal and create a big mess. Place the seal in your freezer or on a gel icepack to chill before you seal your letter.

**3.**

**4.**

Once you've got the hang of it, repeat this process on your good paper or envelope.

Practise beforehand! It's not as easy to get a perfect seal as movies make it seem. Remove your chilled seal from the freezer. Light the sealing wax and, as it begins to melt, position it so it drips onto your paper.

Once the melted wax is roughly the same size as your seal, snuff out the sealing wax and set aside. Resist the temptation to stamp immediately! Wait for 15–20 seconds, then, making sure your seal is perpendicular to the paper, gently press it into the melted wax. Hold for a moment, then lift up the seal; it should come away easily if it was chilled for long enough.

A letter from Beatrix Potter to four-year-old Noel Moore

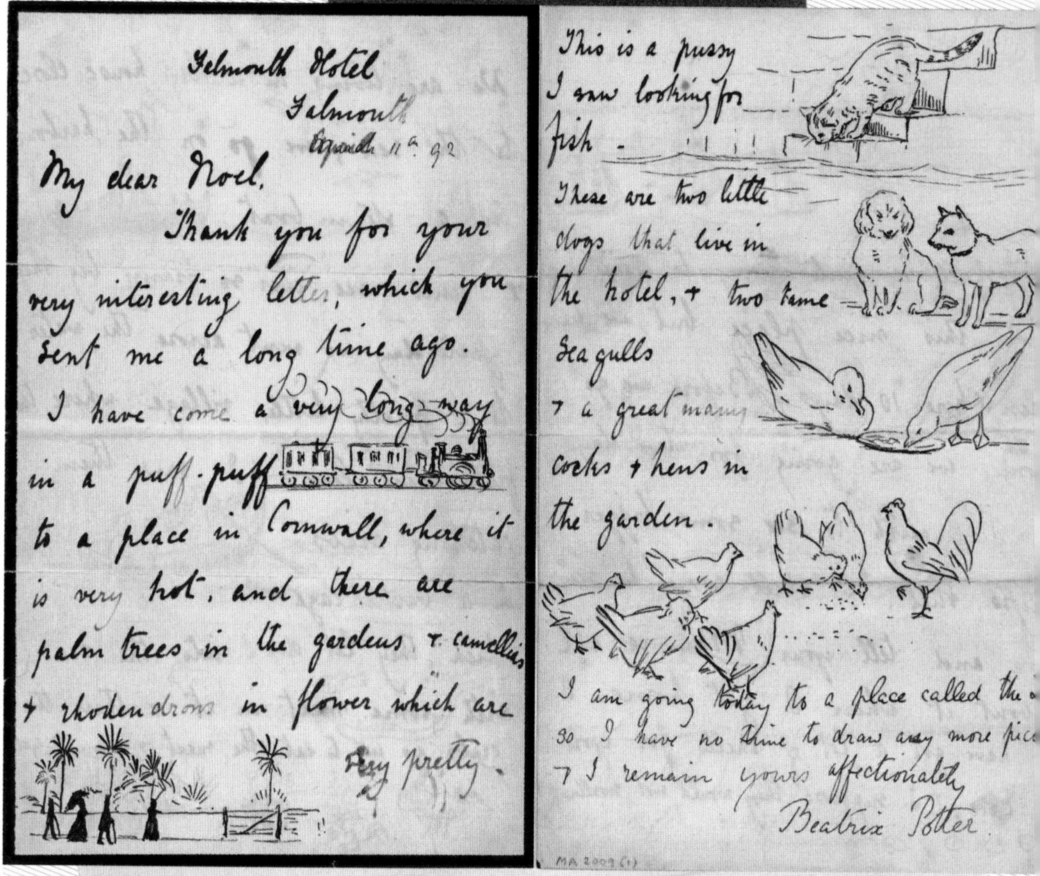

Falmouth Hotel
Falmouth
Aprile 11th 92

My dear Noel,

Thank you for your very interesting letter, which you sent me a long time ago.

I have come a very long way in a puff-puff to a place in Cornwall, where it is very hot, and there are palm trees in the gardens & camellias & rhodendrons in flower which are very pretty.

This is a pussy I saw looking for fish –

These are two little dogs that live in the hotel, & two tame sea gulls & a great many cocks & hens in the garden.

I am going today to a place called the
so I have no time to draw any more pic
& I remain yours affectionately

Beatrix Potter

MA 2009 (1)

My dear Noel,

Thank you for your very interesting letter, which you sent me a long time ago.

I have come a very long way in a puff-puff to a place in Cornwall, where it is very hot, and there are palm trees in the gardens & camellias and rhododendrons in flower which are very pretty.

We are living in a big house close to the sea, we go on the harbour in a steam boat and see ever so many big ships.

Yesterday we went across the water to a pretty little village where the fishermen live. I saw them catching crabs in a basket cage which they let down into the sea with some meat in it & then the crabs go in to eat the meat & cannot get out.

I shall be quite sorry to come away from this nice place but we have been here 10 days. Before we go home we are going for two days to Plymouth to see some bigger ships still. I shall come to see you and tell your Mamma all about it when I get home. I have got a lot of shells for you & Eric, (I suppose they would not swallow them).

This is a pussy I saw looking for fish.

These are two little dogs that live in the hotel, & two tame seagulls & a great many cocks & hens in the garden.

I am going today to a place called the Lizard so I have no time to draw any more pictures,

& I remain yours affectionately
Beatrix Potter

SNAIL MAIL

Photocopy or scan this design for your maker

Hi

Embossing a beautiful-quality cotton envelope always looks magical.

Weddings or other special occasions are perfect for splashing out on an embossing seal.

# EMBOSSING SEALS

Embossing stationery with your own seal will take your letter-craft to a new level. You can have two kinds of embossers made: plastic or metal, and what you choose really depends on your needs. The metal option is the more expensive of the two, but will perform well with a variety of different paper stocks – especially heavier weights – and will last for a long time. The plastic option works just fine for thinner papers. If your design is complex, the experts will probably recommend opting for metal. I recently bought an embosser with four interchangeable plastic designs; it works really well with regular paper stock, so expensive isn't always best.

Most commonly, an embossing seal features a family crest, a monogram or a symbol of who you are. This logo represents *you*, so think carefully about how you'd like to portray yourself. Do you love a particular animal? Why not get an animal seal made? (A wolf, cat, dog or bunny are all excellent choices.) Even a tree, leaf or flower design would work beautifully. Simple, cute motifs like a bow tie, a moustache, ice-cream or even an old-school cameo of your face in profile would make fantastic statements. Otherwise, you can always break with tradition and design something thoroughly unexpected!

Embossing seals work best with keyline designs and circles. Excessively pointy designs are a real no-no, as the sharp corners will cut all the way through thicker paper stocks. If you really want to include triangles and squares, make sure you soften the corners.

Remember, a strong and simple design is best, and always consult with the person making the embossing seal about the specifications and intricacies.

# MAKE ME!

## Snail male

Try making your own snail male – he's a different kind of penpal! The folds on the back of each one are perfect for tucking a tiny letter into.

YOU WILL NEED

* 15 cm (6 in) origami paper squares, or other paper cut to size
* Scrap paper in colours of your choice, plus stickers, stamps and other pretty things, for decorating
* Glue, for decorating
* 16 cm (6¼ in) square envelopes (optional)
* If you're using paper with different-coloured sides, start with the colour you want as your snail male's hair facing down.

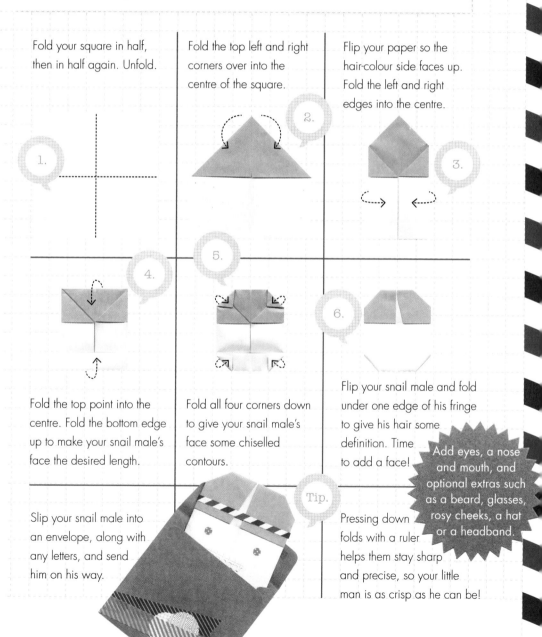

1. Fold your square in half, then in half again. Unfold.

2. Fold the top left and right corners over into the centre of the square.

3. Flip your paper so the hair-colour side faces up. Fold the left and right edges into the centre.

4. Fold the top point into the centre. Fold the bottom edge up to make your snail male's face the desired length.

5. Fold all four corners down to give your snail male's face some chiselled contours.

6. Flip your snail male and fold under one edge of his fringe to give his hair some definition. Time to add a face!

Add eyes, a nose and mouth, and optional extras such as a beard, glasses, rosy cheeks, a hat or a headband.

Slip your snail male into an envelope, along with any letters, and send him on his way.

Tip. Pressing down folds with a ruler helps them stay sharp and precise, so your little man is as crisp as he can be!

Make bunting invitations! Cut out some triangles, decorate and make tracing paper envelopes.

Window-fronted envelopes turn into wonderful invitation holders when you add lots of confetti.

# D.I.Y.
# INVITATIONS

When you have something worth celebrating, whether it's a birthday, a wedding, a house-warming or just your love of parties, homemade invitations are a fun way to bring all of your loved ones together.

Invitations on social media have become the normal way to ask friends and family to attend gatherings. While this is a quick and easy solution, making your own invitations and using old-fashioned correspondence is a fantastic way to get into the spirit of your gathering and have some fun in the process. If you're throwing a themed party, why not make an invitation to match? Take some time out, craft up a storm and surprise your friends and family in the process. Ask your friends to RSVP by post – you may be surprised by the contents of your letterbox before the big day!

If you'd like your invitations to have a layered, handmade feel, but don't have the time to craft an invitation for every one of your guests, make a master invitation and have it professionally copied onto lovely cardstock instead.

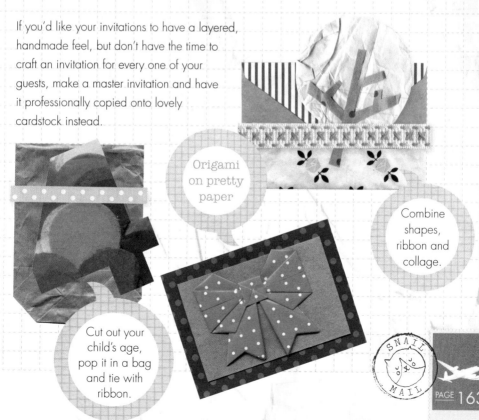

Origami on pretty paper

Combine shapes, ribbon and collage.

Cut out your child's age, pop it in a bag and tie with ribbon.

**MAKE ME!**

# Postable
## peg
## people

This is the perfect project if you want to send a fun surprise in the mail. You can decorate your pegs however you like – try a design that suits the sender. Don't hesitate, get crafting!

* a traditional wooden peg
* washi tape and sticky tape
* small stickers and other decorations like string, sequins or fabric scraps
* a sharp HB pencil
* brown paper or wrapping paper
* a sturdy cardboard tube roughly 12.5 cm (5 in) long and 3 cm (1¼ in) in diameter
* baker's twine or ribbon

Decide what outfit you'd like your person to wear and use washi tape to create it. Wrap each 'leg' of the peg individually for trousers, or both legs together for a skirt. Add string, bow ties and any other embellishments.

Using the HB pencil, draw on a face (you may want to practise on a piece of paper first). Pens bleed if used on wood, so it's best to stick with a good pencil. If you have any tiny stickers, stick on some rosy cheeks.

1.

2.

3.

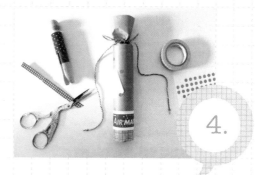
4.

Cut a 20 cm (8 in) square of brown paper. Wrap it around the tube, leaving about 2 cm (¾ in) excess at one end and 5.5 cm (2¼ in) at the other, and secure the long seam with sticky tape. Fold the 2 cm (¾ in) excess over and fasten with sticky tape, then cover the base in washi tape.

Now is your chance to decorate the brown paper, but make sure to leave room for the address. Place your peg person and anything else you are sending into the tube, then use twine or ribbon to tie shut the other end like a bonbon. Ready to pop in the post or hand-deliver!

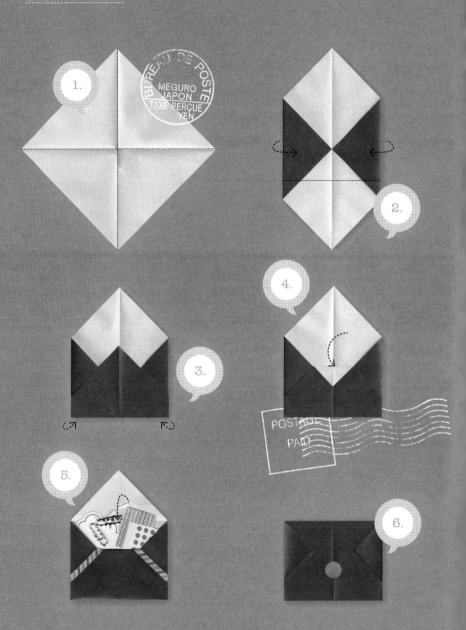

## FLAT-PACKED EXTRAS

Even if you're trying to save on postage, you can still include something special in your envelope. Use your imagination: if it's lightweight, flat (or nearly flat) and can slip comfortably into your envelope, then it's a perfect extra snail mail surprise. Remember, though … just because you *can* send it, doesn't mean you should.

### APPROVED ITEMS

* pressed flowers and leaves
* coasters or business cards of places you've visited together
* confetti
* feathers and other fun nature keepsakes
* bookmarks
* drawings
* photographs

### UNAPPROVED ITEMS

* a lock of hair; if you and the recipient aren't on the same page, you might come across as a stalker (and certainly don't include hair from anywhere that's not your head; see 'Dear catastrophe girlfriend' below)
* underwear (see above)
* the kind of photographs you wouldn't want to be shared
* anything that someone might consider violent, frightening or confusing

### DEAR CATASTROPHE GIRLFRIEND
What *not* to include in your letter

Lady Caroline Lamb included a tuft of her pubic hair in a letter to Lord Byron. Suffice it to say, the relationship didn't end well. Consider your flat-packed extras carefully.

sequins

mini umbrellas

stamps

pressed leaves

paper art

cute paperclips

buttons

Tina sends polaroids

Sarah sends flags

origami

SNAIL MAIL

PAGE 171

MAKE ME!

Pressed

flowers

* **Flowers, petals or leaves (or all three)**
  Whether you pick, gather or buy, choose the best leaves, petals and blooms you can find. And if you've got your eye on your neighbour's garden, ask before you take.

* Scissors
* **2 pieces of paper**
* **Heavy books**

**1.**

Select the flowers you are going to press. Some flowers may be pressed whole, while others may work best if you press the petals or leaves only. The best candidates are freshly bloomed, bright in colour and have thin petals or flowers that can lie flat.

**2.**

Cut the pieces of paper down to size, so they fit inside one of the books with very little overhang.

If you're not sure, experiment away (I press at least one thing per week)!

**3.**

Open one of your books to the middle and place one piece of paper on either the left or right page. Lay your flowers, leaves or petals on the paper, making sure they don't touch each other. Place the other piece of paper on top and shut the book. Weight this down with additional heavy books.

**4.**

Check on your pressed beauties every 2 days and change the paper, which will have absorbed moisture. They should be ready in 2 weeks. Fold into a beautifully written letter and pop into the post, or use some of your pressed flowers to make your own paper (see page 78).

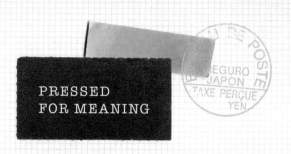

## PRESSED FOR MEANING

### VICTORIAN FLORIOGRAPHY: SENDING MESSAGES WITH FLOWERS

Why not press some of the flowers below and include a little description of each flower's meaning in your letter? If your chosen flower is not easily pressed, a little drawing or photograph with a few words is still pretty and meaningful.

AZALEA
Take care, look after yourself

BLUEBELL
Thank you

CARNATION
I'm fascinated by you, and I love you

CHRYSANTHEMUM
Cheer up!

CLOVER
Be mine (four-leaf); Think of me (flower)

JONQUIL
I return your affections

MAIDENHAIR FERN
Our love is secret

PEONY
I'm too shy to say it, but I like you

PURPLE HYACINTH
I'm sorry

RED ROSE
I love and respect you

SWEET PEA
Goodbye

WHITE LILY
I love spending time with you

writing got worse, the big round
deflation, the word beginning to run into
Costa held closer to the little la scraping
up his eyes.

'If I could the money by public enger on
Thursday it wo be all right at not after then It would
be unnecessary to trouble you If I am sorry to ask you
to lend me this money beca no right to ask you.'
Here Elena had written As ever Your
end who clasps you y the hand', but she had
his out and added a P.S.
can find the aforementioned money by Thursday
I will come back there if you like or we will go to the other
place you said about Money must be to hand by stated
day because Friday is m off for month and I must
have it by th f unab this I may be ab to see
you again but don't know.'

Squeezed in the bottom corner she h written, 'I
send you a tight hug, which she had nev written before.
As usual there was no signature.

Costa re-read the letter twice, searching for hidden
meanings, finding the second reading more frightening
than the first, and the third reading still worse. She must
have stolen her employer, Perhaps her
father's sick again. There was no what anybody
would do once they were exposed big town's infec-
tion. The evil of the city was recogn ed by all toilers of
the land or sea as limitless. People forced to live there for
only a short t ere prone to undergo a kind of bewitch-
ment, from y recovered as soon a unicipal
duties shed, at the town's ir assed on

170

modelled out of sea-she s and coral. This treasure, which
she supposed to be the comp ation for the hardship of
living in houses, she reluctantly abandoned, as being too
beautiful to be of value. Here he only clock had been
emptied of its works, and she was just about to give up
her search when she happened to lift he corner of the sail
and found the wireless set. At st she was doubt d
whether it was worth taking. ere were few impress ve
knobs, and n ing. Then she picked up the head-
p critically scrutinizing their curved
plastic d chromium plating, and thinking:
surely e worth ten pesetas of anybody's

So she e set out of its hiding-place
a length o ce ied it up and carrie of the
low balcony. On one side of the alian bomb
had left a square of desolati noid en brick, the
polished, negroid limbs of cactus, and a little moonlight.
Into this she most carefully lowered her find.

Just before the lift ean-edged as drop-
curtain from the sea, t to the hous an
called Pablo and nim by pelting his eau
window with han nes. Pablo was ex-
politician who afte f manœuvrings and
manipulations had secu parliamentary seat as an
independent radical, on a amme of advan d social
reform, just before the out of the National Move-
ment had abolished parlia y democracy. Since
then he had turned his back o ition. In the summer
season he now earned a sparse ng by standing abso-
lu f e pesetas an hou got up to look like a

175

The wonderful thing about snail mail is that it's more than just posting a letter or receiving one in your own mailbox. You can expand your knowledge of the world and build relationships with like-minded penfriends, sharing inspiration across neighbourhoods or even borders; and you can incorporate messages from your loved ones into your home décor with a little ingenuity.

# 6.
## Getting the most from your post

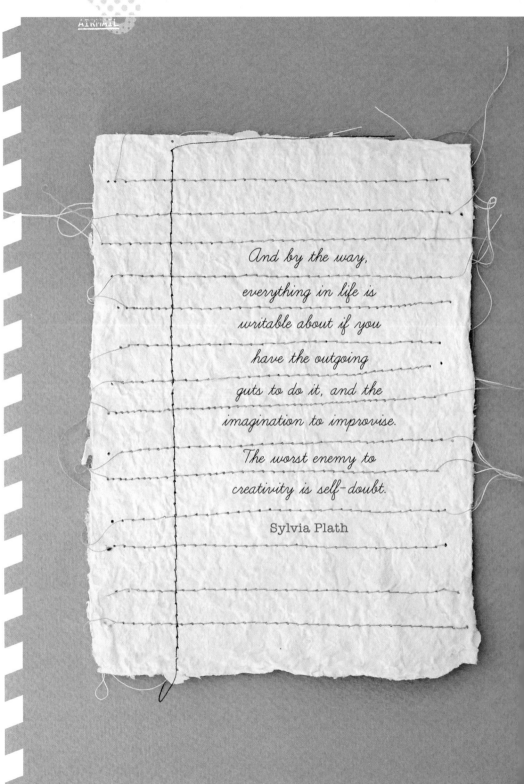

And by the way,
everything in life is
writable about if you
have the outgoing
guts to do it, and the
imagination to improvise.
The worst enemy to
creativity is self-doubt.

Sylvia Plath

When I was in primary school, I had two French penfriends. The first one I wrote to passed me on to her friend, because she thought we'd have more in common! I loved the idea of learning about a different culture and the life of someone my age on the other side of the world. There is something so wonderful about receiving a slice of life in the mail.

*Joe*

PAR AVION

Connecting with like-minded people in other countries, states or neighbourhoods can be really fun. People with similar interests can be found through school, work, family or while on holiday – you just need to look! You can also seek out connections with people in other countries, states or even suburbs on social media.

I enjoy creating fun, themed handmade letter kits to send to friends around the globe. It always puts a smile on my face when I receive a reply in the post – a wonderful surprise in a beautiful and brightly decorated envelope. My penfriend Ishtar lives in Southhampton, in the United Kingdom, and she asked to be my penfriend after discovering my blog *My Life As A Magazine*. We have bonded over a shared love of neon pink, polka dots, Japan and handmade paper paraphernalia. I'm honoured to be Ishtar's penfriend; each of her letters is a work of art that includes envelopes decorated with self-imagined *kawaii* (cute) characters and prints from her hand-carved rubber stamps. Thanks for being a wonderful penfriend, Ishtar – many happy mail days to you!                                            Jenna Templeton

My lovely penfriend Makiko lives in Iwate Prefecture, in Japan. We met on Instagram over a love of *kawaii*, cats and indie music. Because we both love making things, we started sending each other little parcels. Now, whenever my partner Steve and I are in Tokyo, Makiko meets up with us for a special day out – usually one we have planned months in advance! I always look forward to her letters, handwriting and stories about her life in Japan. Thank you for being my friend and penfriend, Makiko!  Michelle Mackintosh

## June & Estella

### Penfriends for over 50 years

In the wake of the Great Depression, at a time when distance truly made communication difficult, many community organisations had programs that connected like-minded girls and boys living on opposite sides of the world. Like many children in the 1930s, June and Estella became penfriends through their local churches.

Even though both came from English-speaking countries, in many ways their worlds were very different: June came from an Anglo-Australian family and was an only child, growing up in the working-class, inner-city Melbourne suburb of Richmond with her mother and grandmother; Estella's family was of Ukrainian heritage and she lived with her parents and siblings in the small paper-mill town of Berlin, New Hampshire.

While most penfriend correspondence tends to peter out as people grow older and life becomes more complex, theirs was a friendship that spanned seven decades, several wars and countless presidents and prime ministers. Through letters, cards and photos, June and Estella witnessed from afar as each grew from teenage girls on the cusp of adulthood to mothers and, in turn, grandmothers several times over. There were marriages, divorces, weddings, funerals, moving houses, retirement: all the stuff of life.

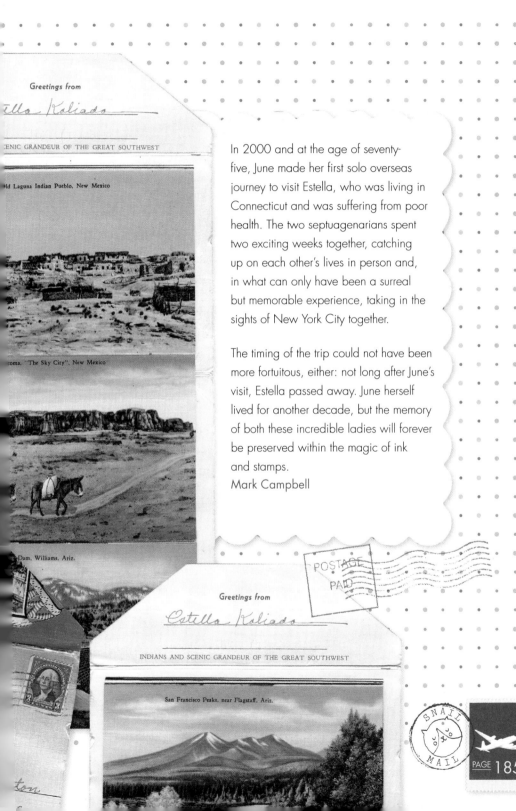

Greetings from

_Estella Kaliada_

SCENIC GRANDEUR OF THE GREAT SOUTHWEST

Old Laguna Indian Pueblo, New Mexico

coma, "The Sky City", New Mexico

Dam, Williams, Ariz.

In 2000 and at the age of seventy-five, June made her first solo overseas journey to visit Estella, who was living in Connecticut and was suffering from poor health. The two septuagenarians spent two exciting weeks together, catching up on each other's lives in person and, in what can only have been a surreal but memorable experience, taking in the sights of New York City together.

The timing of the trip could not have been more fortuitous, either: not long after June's visit, Estella passed away. June herself lived for another decade, but the memory of both these incredible ladies will forever be preserved within the magic of ink and stamps.
Mark Campbell

POSTAGE PAID

Greetings from

_Estella Kaliada_

INDIANS AND SCENIC GRANDEUR OF THE GREAT SOUTHWEST

San Francisco Peaks, near Flagstaff, Ariz.

ton

I turned twenty-three the week before I left for England in 1977. The idea was to live there for at least two years, to travel through Europe, and to visit all the aunties, uncles and cousins I had never met – the ones my parents had left behind when they immigrated to Australia in the fifties, leaving a war-torn, bombed-out London for a better life by Port Phillip Bay.

The world was a much simpler place thirty-seven years ago and, compared to today, was very old-fashioned when it came to communication and keeping in touch with people: no email, no mobile phones and no computers. Everything was slow and apprehensive; now it's frenetically instant.

The fastest form of communication was the humble dial-up telephone, and making international calls was prohibitively expensive for a starving artist like me. Mum called me on special occasions, like birthdays, and only for ten minutes.

Instead, I religiously wrote letters to my family. I probably wrote to someone close at least once a week, spending time to cover the airmail envelope in images of anything that came to mind, or illustrating it with fragments of Old Masters and Impressionist paintings in coloured pencil – sometimes with elaborate borders, but not enough to annoy the postie! At the time, I did worry that the letters wouldn't be delivered, with the name and address so hard to decipher, drowned in coloured pencil as it was.

My beautiful, thoughtful sister Helen hoarded all my letters and fancy envelopes in a paper bag and 'saved them for later'. My other beautiful, thoughtful sister, Frances, has done the same, keeping them in her bottom drawer.

The world of the late seventies, eighties and early nineties seems so long ago. I now call my beloved sisters and Mum on my smart phone, and it would only rarely occur to me to write them a letter on featherweight paper and place a beautiful stamp on it.

I can, however, say that I have saved all of the letters my sisters, brother and Mum sent me. They are stored in a shoebox in a cupboard at the museum where I work, ready to be read, to evoke happy and sad times past. Jane Hyland

## SOCIAL MEDIA, PENFRIENDS AND SNAIL MAIL

I have mixed feelings about social media, but even I can admit it has its benefits! The key is to make sure you find a forum you are comfortable with.

Whichever platform you prefer, social media can be a great place to meet like-minded people, and can provide a springboard for friends to start a relationship outside of the digital world. Social media is also helpful for making new connections if you have moved to a new country or city, and if you are bilingual, then you have twice as many potential friends available to you.

I prefer visual social media sites, like Pinterest and Instagram, as they can give you a forum to show off your snail mail, not to mention provide a wonderful source of inspiration. You can follow and connect with other visually minded people who make or do something you admire. Use your account like an online visual diary, and post interesting images of things that mean something to you, or keep track of projects or ideas you want to follow up on. Don't forget to revisit your old posts once in a while – you might be surprised and inspired by what you find.

## PO BOX 26

SNAIL MAIL

As part of the making of this book, I set up a post office box and invited family, friends and Instagram followers to decorate a letter or envelope and send it to me. I asked that everyone address the envelope with their own name, so when we included the letters in the book, their name would appear on the pages. The result was overwheming.

I received so many beautiful letters, made new friends and was overwhelmed with the kindness and creativity of everyone involved. Letters arrived daily from Australia, the United States, Canada, Hong Kong, Japan, New Zealand and Wales. I received letters from people of all ages – and dogs and cats. I read letters about people's lives, was given beautiful drawings, craft supplies, photographs and so much more. The staff members at my local post office were equally excited to talk about all the decorated letters and to show me new stamp designs.

Whenever you see PO Box 26 on an envelope throughout this book, it's a letter someone has sent me. To everyone involved: thank you from the bottom of my heart!

DISPLAYING
AND STORING
YOUR SNAIL
MAIL

Your snail mail doesn't have to gather dust in a box stashed under the bed. Those beautiful letters and stamps, with their nostalgic feel and whisperings of friendships and love, need to be taken care of, whether that means carefully storing them, or giving them pride of place in your home.

## STORING OLD LETTERS

When it comes to storing your snail mail, you want to make sure that light, moisture and general mishandling don't damage your treasures. Store your letters lying horizontally, so they won't get bent. Particularly old or fragile letters should be kept somewhere cool, dry and dark. A good-quality box tied with ribbon will protect your letters from physical wear and tear, but if you want to take it a step further, photography and paper stores sell archival-quality boxes that are acid- and lignin-free. If you are particularly worried about a letter degrading with age, you can purchase archival mist, a product that prevents paper deterioration.

If you are not too concerned about preserving your personal snail mail for centuries, you can get a little more creative with your storage solutions. A dedicated drawer for your letters is a lovely idea. Perhaps sort the letters by sender or theme, and tie them up with string or ribbon ... you could even label them with cute name tags!

## BRINGING THE OUTSIDE IN

A vintage letterbox is a lovely way to both store and display your treasured letters at home. Make it part of your decor: hang it on a wall, or rest it on a table or bench. You could also craft up a more utilitarian letterbox and let your creativity run free.

An indoor letterbox doesn't just have to be storage, either. Installing a letterbox in your child's bedroom means they can write to Father Christmas, the Easter Bunny, the Tooth Fairy, friends (real or imaginary), or family, and post the letter in their own room. This can help your child open up about their hopes, dreams and fantasies, or even difficult subject matter he or she is comfortable writing and drawing about, but not talking about. Whatever the letter contains, it encourages communication, creative play with words and pictures, and is a great topic for family discussion!

## WOODEN PEGS AND WASHI TAPE

String up some baker's twine and attach your letters with beautiful pegs. If you want to craft the whole look up a notch, use vintage pegs or decorate the sides of your pegs with washi tape.

## HANGERS

Certain styles of vintage coathangers have a felt pad that is perfect for clamping your mail into. Display the coathanger letters on your wall, in and around other artworks.

## RIBBONS

There's not much else prettier than a bundle of beautiful letters tied up with ribbon. Label each bundle with the sender's name or a description of the occasion.

## PEGBOARD

This idea is so wonderful, as you get to display your letters alongside the materials you make them with. Colourful washi tape, scissors, ribbons and twine all make for a beautiful display.

# MAKE ME!

## Crafted-up letterbox

Collage up a store-bought letterbox! Grab a paintbrush and some PVA (Elmer's) glue, and get to beautifying a generic mailbox with some lovely envelopes, stamps, and the like. Put it somewhere prominent to style up your house!

I tore my envelopes rather than cut them. I love the beauty in the imperfection of this technique.

For maximum impact, glue some stamps onto your letterbox.

Why not cover your letterbox with airmail letters or vintage book or magazine pages?

With these airmail letters, I cut out the blue and red stripes and placed them separately.

You can put a layer of matte varnish over your paper-crafted letterbox for longevity.

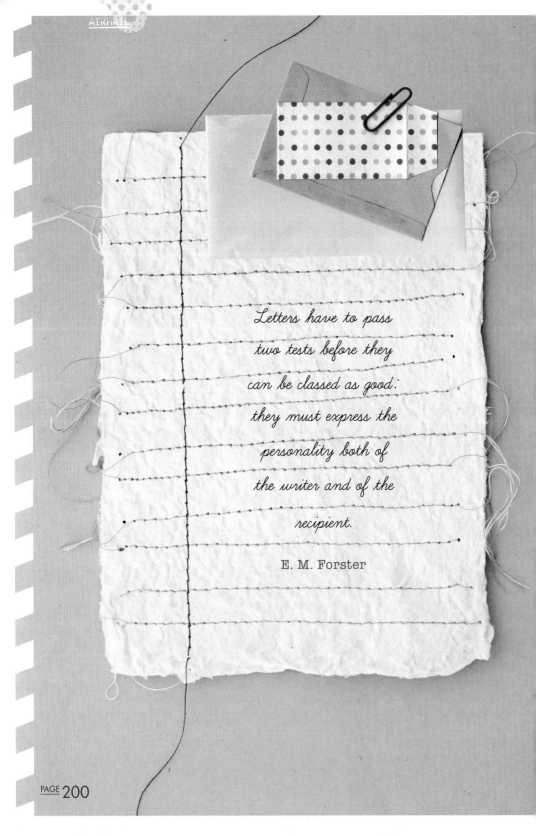

Letters have to pass
two tests before they
can be classed as good:
they must express the
personality both of
the writer and of the
recipient.

E. M. Forster

Use washi tape to cover your letterbox. I used MT Casa, a thicker washi tape used for walls.

OPEN ME

PAGE 201

To Beattie
Wishing you a Happy Birthday
From Alma

To Mother
with the Best of
and heaps of L

**With Best Wishes**

To *Ivor My Darling Wife*

From *four Loving Husband*

Bros.

1334

TO MOTHER

GOOD-LUCK

To Beaty —
Wishing you
every Happiness
Nellie

Wedding

With Best Wishes
from Gracie

...nice & Bert.
...you both, every
...& Success.
...future life.

...M + H. Hughan

CANADA
N.AMERICA
S.AMERICA

No Distance e'er
can wear away esteem
long rooted,
And no chance remove,
the Dear Remembrance
of those we love.
Southey

## REMEMBRANCE OF THINGS PAST

Old letters can lead you on a nostalgic wander through your family history – or the history of strangers. If you're like me and collect old letters and postcards from flea markets, the reading experience can be pretty eye-opening ... if you can make out the handwriting!

Letters fascinate me from a historical perspective. They are a wonderful window into how a life was lived, and how a certain era was experienced. Old letters highlight changes in language, the popularisation of words, the urgencies and trivial moments of the time period, and provide a fantastic observation of functioning relationships. Those of us who have letters our parents and grandparents wrote know it's a curious thing to look into the letter-writing of someone you know well, especially when it's from a different period in their lives. It can be hard to imagine our parents as teenagers, falling in love, or having difficulties. Letters can humanise a person, and give us an insight not possible if pen had not been put to paper.

Letters can be important mementos a person keeps close their whole life. Letters speak of being wanted, needed, loved and special. They also articulate things like 'this did happen', 'I was feeling this way', 'it did matter'.

If a loved one is not with you anymore, a piece of their personality exists in the letters they wrote to you. These keepsakes are some of the most treasured items you could possibly own. Their turn of phrase, their handwriting, the pen they chose and the paper they used all speak of who this person was and what they stood for.

Letters can also help rekindle long-term relationships. Reading old letters can stir the deep feelings or the strong connection you shared with your friend, lover or family member. Revisiting old correspondence may help you rethink a current stand-off and get a relationship back on track.

Writing a letter can bring out the very best in a person or a relationship. The act of writing requires reflection – especially if it concerns a sensitive situation. Things a person is too embarrassed or ashamed to say in person can be thoughtfully articulated – and for better or worse, these sincere expressions are forever preserved on paper. Letter-writing is powerful: in the way it allows us to express ourselves, in the way it preserves our memories, and in the way it makes us feel, long after the ink has dried on those treasured words.

# COLLECTING
# STAMPS

I have always been obsessed with miniatures. My favourite part of the Victoria and Albert Museum in London is the miniatures section, with its tiny paintings in lockets and other precious trinkets. To me, a stamp is the perfect miniature: something functional that everyone can afford. I love their link with a year, a generation, and the popular culture, politics and colour palette of the day.

I have a stamp collection from when I was a kid – so does my husband Steve – and I've been buying stamps on Etsy and eBay for years. I choose stamps from eras in design I love, or ones that feature a subject close to my heart (cats, butterflies, anything to do with nature). Themes like Christmas and the Olympics are pretty special to me, from a design and cultural point of view: I love the way different countries celebrate the same idea in new and exciting ways.

You can of course keep your stamp collections locked away in a cupboard or under your bed, but why not give them the design treatment they deserve, and frame or display them in a pretty way?

POLSKA

2000 zł

POLSKA

2500 zł

POLSKA

3500 zł

BUY A FRAME AND
CATEGORISE YOUR STAMPS
ACCORDING TO ...

* country
* colours (reds and oranges; blues and greens)
* subject matter (animals, insects, boats)
* special events (the Olympics, a centenary, Christmas)

DISPLAY IN A BEAUTIFUL BOX OR
DRAWER

SCAN IN YOUR STAMPS AND
MAKE WRAPPING PAPER:
ARRANGE YOUR STAMPS ON
YOUR SCANNER BY COLOUR,
SIZE OR SHAPE

BUY A CUTE FRAME THAT
SANDWICHES YOUR STAMPS
BETWEEN TWO LAYERS OF GLASS

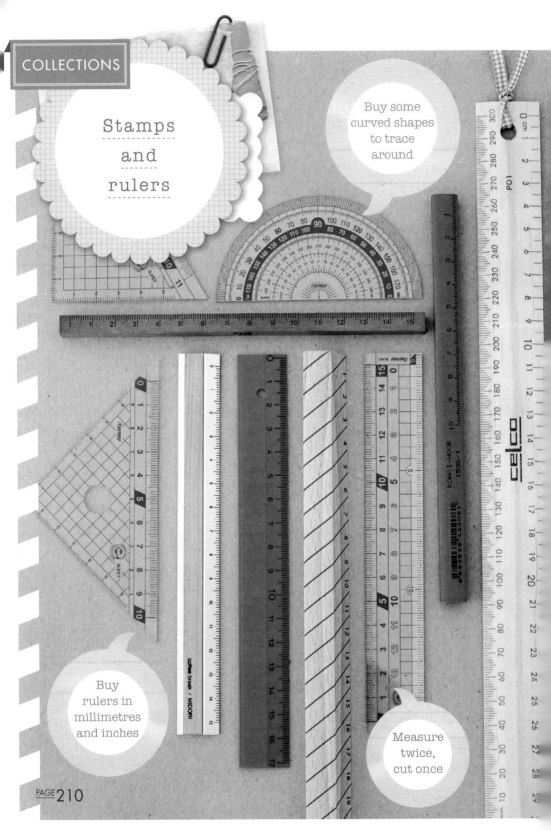

Stamps
and
rulers

Buy some
curved shapes
to trace
around

Buy
rulers in
millimetres
and inches

Measure
twice,
cut once

Colour code your stamps!

Here you'll find all of the templates you need to create your own mail art masterpieces. You can enlarge or reduce them to any size on a photocopier, then decorate them to your heart's content. Be bold and get creative!

# Templates

# SELF-LOCKING AEROGRAM
## TEMPLATE

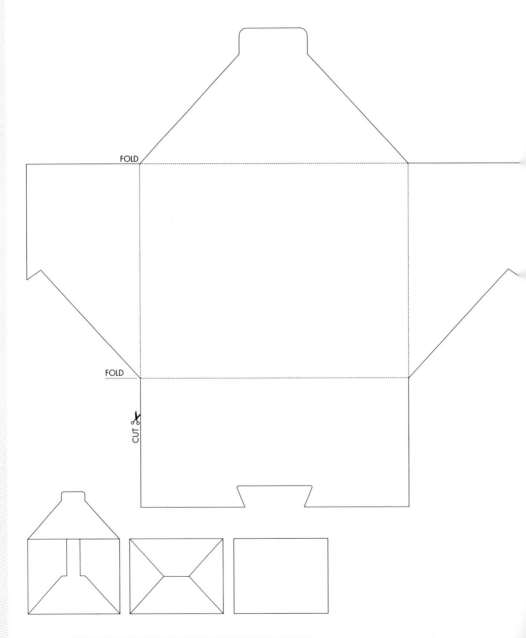

FOLD

FOLD

CUT

PHOTOCOPY AND CUT. TEMPLATE CAN BE BLOWN UP TO ANY SIZE

AIR-MAIL

SEND YOUR HERE

V···— MAIL

See Instruction
No. 5

V···— MAIL

Make envelopes out of vintage paper and packaging

Bags make great envelopes

Collect eras or brands

Flea markets are a great place to start

Fleischerei

# FOLD-AND-GLUE
## AEROGRAM TEMPLATE

FOLD

FOLD

FOLD

FOLD

CUT

FOLD

PHOTOCOPY AND CUT. TEMPLATE CAN BE BLOWN UP TO ANY SIZE

NEKO-GRAM TEMPLATE
(FOLD AND GLUE)

FOLD

FOLD

FOLD

CUT OUT AND GLUE THE WRONG SIDES
OF THE NEKO-GRAM PIECES TOGETHER

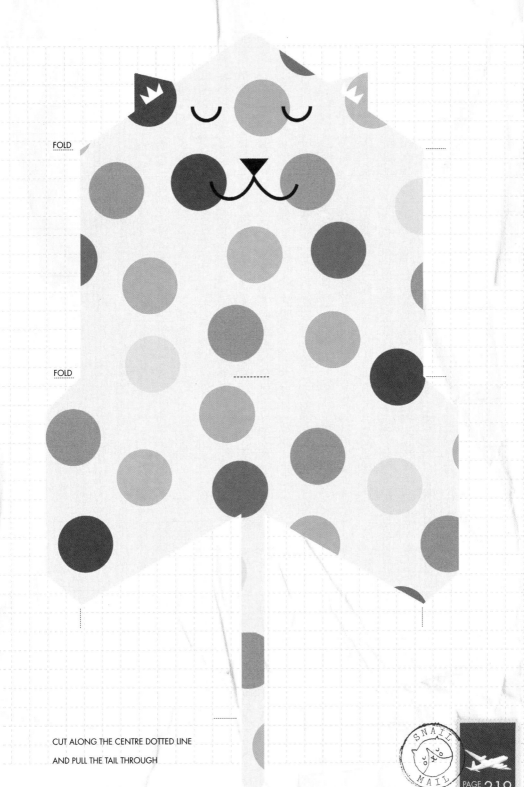

FOLD

FOLD

CUT ALONG THE CENTRE DOTTED LINE
AND PULL THE TAIL THROUGH

# FABRIC ENVELOPE TEMPLATE
## (FOLD AND SEW)

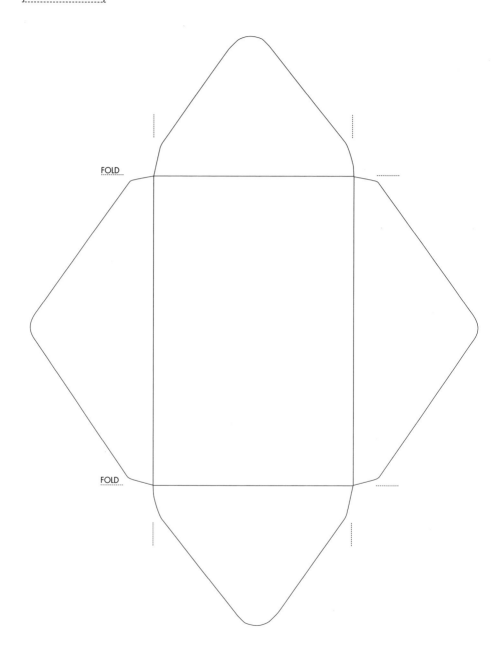

FOLD

FOLD

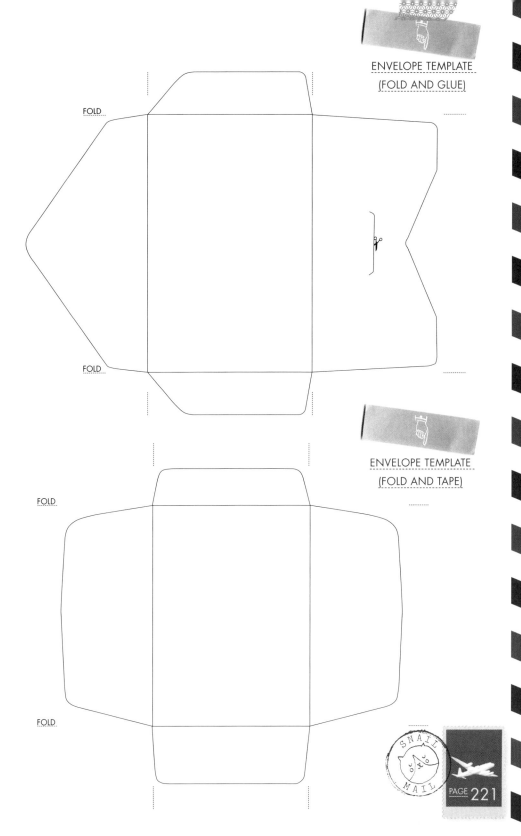

ENVELOPE TEMPLATE
(FOLD AND GLUE)

FOLD

FOLD

ENVELOPE TEMPLATE
(FOLD AND TAPE)

FOLD

FOLD

SNAIL MAIL

# THANK YOU

Thank you to mine own dear-heart, Steve Wide. Not only for all of your love, support and ideas, but also for putting up with a house that looked like a mashup of craft heaven and craft hell, and for cooking for me every single night for three months. //

Thank you so much to Hardie Grant, in particular my publisher Paul McNally, for all your support and for believing in my idea. I feel honoured and blessed to be a Hardie Grant author. // To Rihana Ries, a wonderful editor and amazing snail-mail contributor: really, thank you for everything. // Thank you to Mark Campbell, for your creative genius, and for bringing cakes to the photoshoot at the most crucial moment. // Thank you to Chris Middleton, for your absolutely exceptional photography, and for the long hours you put into this project. //

To my father: the letter you wrote me was the inspiration for this book. I wish you were here to see it published; I miss you every day. // Thank you to my family: Mum, Andrew, Dee, Olive and Leo; Carolyn, Evie and Velvet; and Stephen and Paul. // Thank you to my incredibly supportive friends – Jane and William, May, Sylvie, Olivia and Joel, Melinda, Pacquita, Graham, Trisha, Beci and Alice, Dawn, Steve and Ingrid, Heather, Hiki, Makiko, and Kate – for all your encouragement, help, ideas and love during the making of this book. //

Thank you to Heather Menzies, for express-posting your stamp collection to me, and for your enthusiasm and creativity – not to mention your help and support, including all your immaculate late-night/early-morning artwork and calligraphy. // Thank you to Alice Oehr, for your help on the photoshoot – and so much more. // Thank you to Jane Ormond, for letting me borrow your old letters and for constantly listening to all of my ideas. // Thank you to Pip for lending me your wonderful vintage typewriter. // Thank you to my penfriend Makiko, for sharing your stamp collection with me. // Thank you to Hiki, for letting me photograph your grandfather's amazing stamp collection in Tokyo. // Thank you to Laura McKellar, for organising Helen McKellar and Jane Hyland's wonderful story; to Mark Campbell, for organising June Campbell and Estella Sholomicky's wonderful story; and to Jenna and Ishtar. // And last but not least, from the bottom of my heart, thank you to all the people who spent time and love making letters and mail art for PO Box 26. //

# THE PO BOX 26 LETTER-WRITERS

Abby Salter
Alice Oehr
Amanda & Emma
Amanda Paino
Amy Devereux
Amy Di Stasio
Andy Xie
Anette Wagner
Ann Monzon
Ann Nguyen/Akira Belle
Adeline, Chester and
 Humphrey (RIP)
Beci Orpin
Blank Goods
Bianca Jagoe
Ari Rashid & Sofia Davis
Carolyn O'Neill
Cat, Abbey & Zoe Tranter
Catherine Insch
Chanie Stock, Ponie,
 Nancy & Honey Curtis
Chizuru Taguchi
Chris Kerruish
Cintia Gonzalez-Pell
Coco Tashima
Deb Baker
Dawn-Ellen Wood
Emily Ridgway
Emma Jay
Esther Olsson
Flora Waycott
Fur Hairdressing
Gizelle Bongiorno

Graham Moss
Heather Jane Menzies
Helena Leslie
Hiki Komura
Ingrid Josephine
Jacinta Mustica
Jane & Marcus
Jane Ormond
Jas Ronny
Jenna Templeton
Jess Racklyeft
Jesse-Bree
Justine Betts
Kat Chadwick
Karen
Kelly Lear
Kimberlee Fuller
Kimberley-Jayne
Lamina, Doabit
Le Dee Ma Petto & Ta Saki
 Kumi Ko & Lady Muppet
Leah Gullan, Milly & Alice
Louise Mulhall
Lydia, Peace Love and
 Pom Poms
Magdalena Franco
Makiko Sugita
Mark Campbell
Meg Salter
Melinda Wansbrough
 & Audrey Player
Michele Luminato
Mordie the dog

Nadine Mari
Nani Puspasari
Neryl Walker
Niina Aoki
Nina & Clare
Old School, New School
Olive & Leo Mackintosh
Pacquita Maher
Peader Thomas
Rebecca Kate
Renee Dare
Rihana Ries
Rin Dawson
Rose DeAngelis
Sarah Deboice
Senator Wigstock
Shalimma Althaus
Sharny Yoko
Sheridan Forde
Shoko Seko
Steph Ransom & Polly
 Bennetiz
Stephanie O'Brien & Frida
Stephen Banham
Steve Wide
Susan Fitzgerald
Tara Broad
Tess McCabe
Tijana Bozic
Tina Thompson
Unleash Creative
William Eicholtz

Published in 2015 by
Hardie Grant Books

Hardie Grant Books (Australia)
Ground Floor, Building 1
658 Church Street
Richmond, Victoria 3121
www.hardiegrant.com.au

Hardie Grant Books (UK)
5th & 6th Floors
52–54 Southwark Street
London SE1 1UN
www.hardiegrant.co.uk

Robert Browning letter reproduced
from the original owned by Wellesley
College, Margaret Clapp Library,
Special Collections.

Beatrix Potter, Vincent van Gogh, Oscar
Wilde and Jane Austen Letters courtesy
The Pierpont Morgan Library/Art
Resource, NY.

A Cataloguing-in-Publication entry is
available from the catalogue of the
National Library of Australia at
www.nla.gov.au

Snail Mail
ISBN 978 1 74270 877 5

Publishing Director: Paul McNally
Editor: Rihana Ries
Design Manager: Mark Campbell
Designer: Michelle Mackintosh
Photographer: Chris Middleton
Production Manager: Todd Rechner

Colour reproduction by Splitting Image
Colour Studio

Printed and bound in China by 1010
Printing International Limited

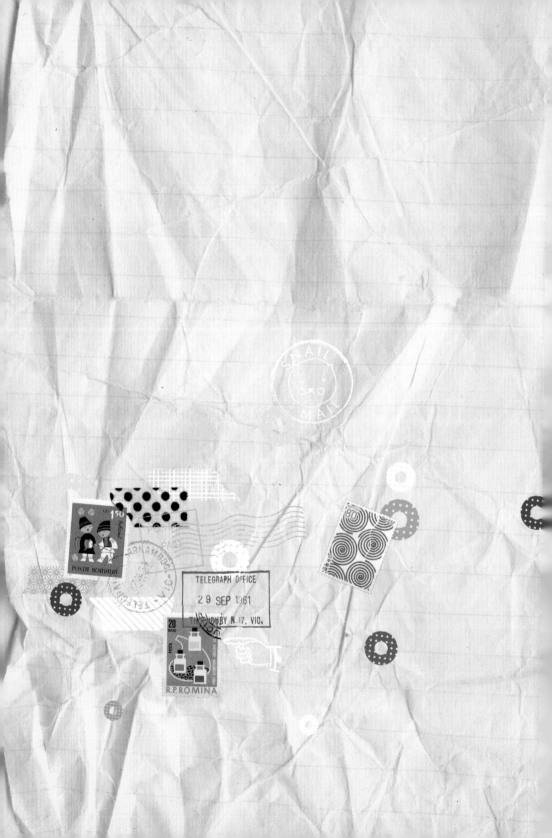